XMAS,S OOPS!

TO MY DARLING GEOFF.

HAPPY FOOTBALL DARLING.

LOVE SYLVIA

PORTSMOUTH
Champions of England
1948-49 & 1949-50

DESERT ISLAND FOOTBALL HISTORIES
www.desertislandbooks.com

Portsmouth: Champions of England – 1948-49 & 1949-50	1-874287-38-4
Portsmouth: From Tindall to Ball – A Complete Record	1-874287-25-2
Stoke City: The Modern Era – A Complete Record	1-874287-39-2
West Ham: The Elite Era – A Complete Record	1-874287-31-7
Bristol City: The Modern Era – A Complete Record	1-874287-28-7
Colchester Utd: Graham to Whitton – A Complete Record	1-874287-27-9
Halifax Town: From Ball to Lillis – A Complete Record	1-874287-26-0
Coventry City: The Elite Era – A Complete Record	1-874287-03-1
Coventry City: An Illustrated History	1-874287-36-8
Luton Town: The Modern Era – A Complete Record	1-874287-05-8
Luton Town: An Illustrated History	1-874287-37-6
Hereford United: The League Era – A Complete Record	1-874287-18-X
Cambridge United: The League Era – A Complete Record	1-874287-32-5
Peterborough United: The Modern Era – A Complete Record	1-874287-33-3
Wimbledon: From Southern League to Premiership	1-874287-09-0
Wimbledon: From Wembley to Selhurst	1-874287-20-1
Wimbledon: The Premiership Years	1-874287-40-6
Aberdeen: The European Era – A Complete Record	1-874287-11-2
The Story of the Rangers 1873-1923	1-874287-16-3
The Story of the Celtic 1888-1938	1-874287-15-5
History of the Everton Football Club 1878-1928	1-874287-14-7
The Romance of the Wednesday 1867-1926	1-874287-17-1
Red Dragons in Europe – A Complete Record	1-874287-01-5
The Book of Football: A History to 1905-06	1-874287-13-9
England: The Quest for the World Cup – A Complete Record	1-897850-40-9
Scotland: The Quest for the World Cup – A Complete Record	1-897850-50-6
Ireland: The Quest for the World Cup – A Complete Record	1-897850-80-8

PORTSMOUTH

CHAMPIONS of ENGLAND 1948-49 & 1949-50

Series Editor: Clive Leatherdale

Colin Farmery

DESERT ISLAND BOOKS

First Published in 2000

DESERT ISLAND BOOKS LIMITED
89 Park Street, Westcliff-on-Sea, Essex SS0 7PD
United Kingdom
www.desertislandbooks.com

British Library Cataloguing-in-Publication Data
A catalogue record for this book is available from the British Library

ISBN 1-874287-38-4

Printed in Great Britain
by
The Cromwell Press, Trowbridge, Wiltshire

Photographs in this book are reproduced courtesy of
The News, Portsmouth

Contents

Page

Preface by Phil Rookes 6
Author's Note 7
Introduction 8

1. Foundations – (1939-1945) 13

2. Return to Normal – (1945-1948) 27

3. Golden Days – (July-November 1948) 43

4. Winter of Content – (December 1948-February 1949) 61

5. At the Double – (February-May 1949) 75

6. The Team to Beat – (May-November 1949) 91

7. Days of Doubt – (November 1949-February 1950) 107

8. Fight to the Finish – (March-May 1950) 121

9. How the Mighty Fell – (Post-1950) 135

Guide to Seasonal Summaries 147

Preface

What is it about Portsmouth Football Club that calls for such pride and devotion from both fans and players? It is difficult to put a finger on it, except to say there is magic there somewhere and this book amply illustrates the fever which gripped fans and players during the Golden Championship Years.

Everyone connected with Pompey contributed to this fantastic period. These were heady days for the players, the majority of whom had just been demobbed after war service. Indeed, the Royal Navy and the Royal Marines nurtured six of those men who helped form the great Portsmouth team of that period. This war service, demanding discipline and close comradeship, transferred itself to the Portsmouth players in peacetime.

In 1946 a bond developed among the players, which reached its peak two years later. They genuinely liked each other, socialised together, accepted discipline from the club and forged a close-knit unit which few, if any, other clubs could match. That bond remains to this day. This was the key to the success of Portsmouth Football Club in those great years, but the wives too played a tremendous part.

Pride in pulling on a Pompey shirt was complete. Walking into the pre-match dressing room and seeing your numbered shirt hanging on the peg, with shorts and stockings draped above, cotton wool squares and laces laid out, the precious boots placed under the seat created a feeling which built up over the next half hour. It was a ritual. One item of gear after another, the frequent face washes and more frequent visits to the loo!

With the referee's bell approaching, boots were carefully laced and stockings tied. Controlled tension built up, followed by the last words from Jim Stewart, Head Trainer, and then it rang. We clip-clopped up the dark passage in our studded boots, captain Reg Flewin at the front with the ball and each player in his favoured position in the line. I was always number three.

Soon a dazzling light would greet the team as they surfaced on to the running track to be greeted by a great roar. Players still find it difficult to describe their feelings emerging from that tunnel. Soon everything settled down as the Milton End was reached. It was always the Milton End, unless the visitors behaved badly and got there first, of course.

These reminiscences provide a few little insights, perhaps, into the pre-match rituals of the Pompey team that was destined for greatness. I am pleased to have the opportunity to write the preface of this excellent book, *Portsmouth: Champions of England*. It reflects this fantastic period in Pompey's history and I wish it every success.

PHIL ROOKES

Author's Note

Portsmouth Football Club and its championship years of 1949 and 1950 are the stuff of legend. Through the dark days of near bankruptcy and Fourth Division football in the late 1970s, the post-war exploits of Jimmy Dickinson and Co sustained the belief, even among those, such as me, who were born long after the event, that Pompey were a 'big' club and their time would come again.

Fifty years on from those championship years, Pompey retain the cachet of a sleeping giant, but as football's finances spiral ever higher, the question has to be whether Portsmouth – or any provincial club for that matter – could ever repeat the feat of winning, let alone retaining the English League title. Jack Walker's fathomless pockets enabled Blackburn to snatch the Premiership in 1995. Subsequent history suggests that will prove to be an aberration in a sport where telephone number figures are now paid to Premiership reserve players.

Portsmouth: Champions of England is a tale from an altogether different world of maximum wages and one-club loyalty that modern professional footballers would have trouble understanding. Supporters of the game will have fewer problems in that respect. The agony and ecstasy of being a fan remains a constant reference point, where referees are blind, the opposition lucky and the club's management inept. This is their story too.

In writing this book, Richard Owen, the Honorary Historian of Portsmouth FC, was a mine of useful information, as ever, while Peter Jeffs demonstrated his deep knowledge of this era of football when correcting my first draft. Phil Rookes, Pompey full-back in the 1948-49 season, added some invaluable insights and wrote the preface. These three people deserve my special thanks.

I am also grateful to former players – goalie Ernie Butler, defender Jimmy Stephen, and inside-forward Len Phillips and his wife Joan, who freely gave their time to speak to me. I assure them the pleasure was all mine. Many supporters from the time also helped extensively, including Cyril Lucas, Betty Rowse, John Phillips (who later played for Pompey), Dave Randall, John Danagher, Alan Hutchings, Mike Barnard, Peter Downton and June Veal. I also appreciated the help of Roger Holmes and Ian White, and Mick Cooper, who made available to me his large collection of photographs. As ever, Di Lloyd, my wife, was a constant support and constructive critic. My publisher and editor Clive Leatherdale also deserves my thanks for proposing this book to me and for accommodating my maverick approach. His attention to detail and quality is an object lesson to all aspiring football publishers.

My dream is that one day this book will have a sequel.

COLIN FARMERY
July 2000

Introduction

Champions of England – Again!

On Saturday, 6 May 1950, shortly after 4.20pm, Portsmouth and England left-half Jimmy Dickinson threaded the ball through the middle of the field at Fratton Park. The pass split the Aston Villa defence in two, allowing makeshift centre-forward Bill Thompson to run on and crash an unstoppable shot past the Villa goalkeeper, Rutherford. The goal put Pompey 4-0 up and, although there were still eighteen minutes to play, it all but ensured that the south-coast club would become the first team since Arsenal in 1935 to retain the League Championship trophy for a second successive season. Pompey needed only to win this game to be certain of doing so. Although second-placed Wolverhampton began the day level on points, and were trouncing Birmingham 6-1 at Molineux, nothing realistically (short of Wolves bagging twenty goals) could threaten Pompey's massive goal-average superiority.

That fourth goal put paid to the last remaining doubts, and the closing minutes saw the Fratton Park crowd of more than 42,000 indulge in celebrations of a kind never yet repeated. The club flag – already bearing the legend 'Champions 1948-49' was hoisted over the South Stand and then, while play continued, the trophy itself was positioned at the front of the stand, by the directors seats, where all those not actually playing might gaze lovingly upon it. This was, surely, the greatest moment in Portsmouth Football Club's proud and eventful 102-year history. Even though the team that took the field that afternoon was shorn of key players through suspension and injury, there was no doubt that the eleven men wearing the royal blue shirts – emblazoned with the famous star and crescent badge – white shorts and red stockings were a cut above any other side in the land. They were simply Champions of England.

The success of the side was largely down to three guiding lights: manager and former chief scout Bob Jackson, head trainer Jimmy Stewart, and former manager Jack Tinn, who had led the club to FA Cup glory in 1939 before parting company in not entirely amicable fashion in 1947. Between them, these three men had demonstrated all their experience and judgment of young football-ers – capitalising on the fact that Portsmouth was a city with extensive naval and army connections – to build a tight-knit group with a team spirit second to none. The popular father figure, Jackson, complemented the tenacious Stewart, who had responsibility for preparing the side for battle each Saturday. The outfit they created truly was a team without stars. It remained that way, even when the international selection committees belatedly woke up to the talents of Dickinson, wingers Peter Harris and Jack Froggatt, and inside-forward Len Phillips. Each of these went on to play for England, while the combative talents of right-half Jimmy Scoular would serve Scotland with distinction.

That team spirit was engendered by the fact that the majority of the squad lived within walking distance of Fratton Park. Centre-forward Duggie Reid lived on Carisbrooke Road, full-back Phil Rookes on Edgeware Road, goalkeeper Ernie Butler in Bonchurch Road, to name but three – all addresses within a couple of decent drop-kicks of the ground. Only Scoular, who commuted from Gosport – and could regularly be seen mounting his cycle to ride home from the ferry – and Dickinson, who continued to live in his home town of Alton in north Hampshire, lived outside the city. The players' wives, too, were a close-knit group, congregating in the South Stand on match days. Often the players and their wives would socialise together, to the theatre or a dance, say, creating a unique spirit and camaraderie that allowed Portsmouth Football Club to become the first – and to this day, only – club south of London to muscle in on the football elite's top table.

Pompey had a reputation for finding and developing footballers that was second to none, through an extensive network of scouts who scoured the land to bring promising talent to the attention of the management. The club's enclosure at Bridgemary, between Fareham and Gosport, was home to Pompey's 'A' team, which played in the Hampshire League. Bridgemary also hosted innumerable trial matches and was the nursery of many a career at Fratton Park, including that of John Phillips, a Portsmouth schoolboy in 1948, who watched his home-town team win the League before going on to play for the first team himself. Star players seeking match fitness after injury would sometimes turn out for the 'A' team, giving a rare treat for local spectators.

In the immediate post-war era, as transfer fees began to snowball – reflecting the huge revenues pouring in from vast crowds – Pompey were almost unique among top division clubs in only once signing a player for more than £10,000. Even then, full-back Jimmy Stephen, who signed in October 1949, wouldn't become a regular fixture in the side until the 1950-51 season. His National Service commitments in the Royal Air Force took precedence over his appearances as a professional footballer.

The entire team that trounced Aston Villa (5-1 was the final score) on that May afternoon had cost a fraction of the then record signing, £26,500, paid by Preston in December 1949 for Sheffield Wednesday's Eddie Quigley. Pompey's most expensive player that day, a £7,500 buy from Stockport, was inside-forward Duggie Reid, who notched a hat-trick. Pompey's other scorer, two-goal stand-in No 9 Bill Thompson, was Glasgow-born and a product of the club's close relationship with the Scottish junior leagues, having signed from Carnoustie in 1946. The Scottish Central League even competed for the 'Pompey Cup', in recognition of the special place occupied by Portsmouth FC in their organisation. Thompson wasn't even a forward. His usual position was at half-back, but the injuries, illnesses and suspensions that had dogged the team had seen him fill in at full-back, centre-half – and now centre-forward – as required.

The Scot found himself playing in this unaccustomed role in such a critical match because, with two games left to play and just two points needed for the title, the Football Association had imposed a fourteen-day ban on right-half Scoular. Added to which, regular centre-forward Ike Clarke had required surgery on an injured toe. Amid mutterings among supporters of an FA 'conspiracy' to try to deny the club their second successive title – Scoular had been sent off 52 long days previously, at Derby – Pompey had also been handicapped by losing regular centre-half Reg Flewin to injury for five weeks. Thompson had occupied Scoular's position in Pompey's penultimate match – a 0-2 defeat at Arsenal on the Wednesday – which meant victory over Villa was imperative. But with Clarke's replacement, Reg Pickett, also out through injury, Thompson's height and presence was seen as the ideal foil for a potent inside-forward pairing of Reid and Phillips and the pace and trickery on the wings of Froggatt and Harris. The return of Flewin against Villa – he had been named in an FA party to tour Canada, leaving the following week – gave the team a boost. And the news that Villa would field Craddock at centre-forward in place of Welsh international Trevor Ford further encouraged Pompey supporters to believe it might be their afternoon and their season. Some of those present at the occasion recall the Villa full-back turning to a section of the Fratton crowd before the start and reassuring them: 'Don't worry, you'll win this.'

Apocryphal or otherwise, it does not matter. The writing was soon on the wall. According to match reports of the time, within twenty seconds of the kick-off the decision to field Thompson at No 9 had paid off. He took a pass from Froggatt and coolly clipped the ball past the goalkeeper. From that moment the title was staying at Fratton Park. Reid doubled the lead after 26 minutes when he returned a poor punch from Rutherford with a trademark thunderbolt shot. Pompey's 2-0 interval lead soon became 3-0 as Dickinson dummied over a free-kick and Reid cracked the ball through a gap in the Villa defence. With that goal, any worries about Wolves' 5-0 half-time lead began to melt away.

Following Pompey's fourth goal the championship trophy was brought out from safe keeping to the directors box to await presentation upon the final whistle. The sight of it, glinting in the sunshine, did not distract Reid from the task of nodding in Froggatt's left-wing cross. Only ten minutes now remained, but the last goal went to the visitors. With time running out, Pompey full-back Bill Hindmarsh handled in the box, allowing Dorsett to convert the penalty. 5-1 it remained, and when the referee blew his whistle it provoked a stampede of Pompey fans, who swarmed onto the pitch to acclaim their heroes for the second time in twelve months.

Britain in the immediate post-war era was a place which, viewed from a distance of half a century, seems like another world. Rationing was still in place and cities like Portsmouth still bore the scars of war, with huge swathes of land little more than scarcely cleared bombsites. However, there was a feeling that after the war, whatever the continuing hardships, peacetime was to be savoured. Football was one of the prime beneficiaries, with supporters flooding through the turnstiles in unprecedented numbers.

Not that professional footballers benefited materially from the phenomenal popularity of the game. In August 1948 the Football League narrowly averted a players' strike over wages, and at the start of the following season the celebrated forward Wilf Mannion found himself enmeshed in a protracted contract dispute with his club, Middlesbrough. The maximum wage was still in place and although most players were better off than the average working man, perks such as the free bus rides enjoyed by Len Phillips on corporation buses, for example, hardly put these men into the super-tax bracket. This story is a tale of talented footballers but otherwise ordinary men, who lived among the people who watched them on a Saturday afternoon. Supporter Cyril Lucas from Gosport recalls that one Saturday morning in the late 1940s he came across a group of men kicking a ball about on Southsea Common. That 'group of men' was actually the Stoke City side 'relaxing' before the fixture at Fratton Park in the afternoon. The Pompey players were used to walking to the ground on a match-day – car-driving was prohibited during the playing season – arriving three-quarters of an hour before kick off.

There was no doubt that a civility among players and supporters existed in a way which is hard today for anyone under the age of fifty to fully understand. Referees were respected and their word on the field of play was largely unchallenged law. To be booked was rare and to be sent off a disgrace, but to paint a nostalgic, rose-tinted picture would be inaccurate and unrealistic. Football was a hard game then and had its share of uncompromising characters. To be tackled by the tenacious Jimmy Scoular could leave an indelible impression on mind and body, and match reports from those days revealed players were far from beneath a sly tug of the shirt or deliberate handball if the situation warranted it. However, as Phil Rookes, Pompey's full-back of the time points out, the tackle from behind was literally unheard of. Players arguably were more sporting, but there was a greater acceptance of the physical side of the game and in that context referees patently applied different standards to today.

Indeed, like today, referees, were widely criticised by the press and supporters. One *Football Mail* article reckoned the standard was lower than ever and supporters were forever dashing off letters to the editor bemoaning referees' partiality when it came to matters Pompey. The modern football supporter would also find the elite in the English game fifty years ago fairly familiar. Arsenal, Manchester United and Liverpool were the big-hitters in the immediate post-war period, with the Gunners of Highbury the cat's cream so far as the Fleet Street press was concerned.

What was different in the world of football in the late 1940s, however, was that a well-run provincial football club had the opportunity to challenge on an equal footing with the big-city giants. Stoke, Blackpool, and Burnley all went close to glory in both the League and FA Cup shortly after the war, while Derby won the Cup in 1946 and regularly held a position in the top five of the table. And then there was Portsmouth. Unlikely Cup winners in 1939, the south-coast club was regarded as unfashionable, unfancied and largely under-rated by almost everyone – until it was too late. This is the remarkable story of an apparently ordinary team, which went on to achieve extraordinary greatness.

1

Foundations

1939 – 1945

The roots of Pompey's championship success are deeply embedded in World War II. It was those years of football's surreal, never-never world of guest players, restricted attendances, erratic fixture lists and even more erratic results that saw the nucleus of the team which was to dominate English football for two seasons take shape. But even as war was declared in 1939, the club had already gone a considerable way towards establishing itself among the elite.

Having been elected to the Third Division in 1920, as the Football League expanded Portsmouth Football Club became the first of that 'new intake' to climb into the First Division. The Third Division (South) championship had been collected in 1924 on the back of 28 goals from centre-forward Billy Haines. Three years later 'Farmer's Boy' – as the West Country-born player was widely known – etched his name into Fratton folklore with a record-breaking forty goals in 42 league matches as Pompey edged out Manchester City by the slenderest of goal-averages for a place in the old First Division.

Under the charismatic yet autocratic management of Jack Tinn, who was appointed manager in June 1927, Pompey established themselves as a solid, if unspectacular First Division team, but one with the happy knack of making their presence felt in the FA Cup. Three times the Pompey Chimes pealed around Wembley before war intervened. In 1929 the team lost 0-2 to Bolton Wanderers, in their first appearance at the twin towers, when their hopes were dashed by an injury to left-back Tommy Bell that left the team depleted. Five years later Manchester City exacted belated revenge for their promotion heartache, scoring twice in the final fifteen minutes to take the Cup. Pompey's injury jinx had struck again, skipper Jimmy Allen having to be carried off with concussion, and the ten men were unable to protect Septimus Rutherford's first-half goal. That final was notable, too, because City's 19-year-old goalkeeper, Frank Swift, fainted on the final whistle.

It was the 1938-39 FA Cup campaign, however, which established once and for all Pompey's cup-fighting reputation. Enjoying kind luck with the draw – which gave Pompey a home tie in every round – the team strode to the semi-final at Highbury where they survived a tense affair against Huddersfield. That game had the distinction of being the first occasion that teams wore shirts numbered 1-11 in a club (as opposed to international) fixture, adding another curious 'first' to the Pompey story. Among their other more quixotic records was taking part in the first match (versus Newcastle in 1931) not to feature a single corner-kick.

For most of the Highbury semi-final Pompey trailed to a Bobby Barclay goal, but their Wembley dream was revived when goals from Bert Barlow and 'Jock' Anderson in the last fifteen minutes broke Huddersfield's hearts. Their opponents in the final were Wolves, managed by Major Frank Buckley, red-hot favourites and supposedly given an additional edge by their controversial use of 'monkey-gland' injections – although Pompey's players had also received the dubious benefit of these jabs – which allegedly enhanced performance. *En route* to Wembley, Wolves had scored nineteen goals and conceded just three, and in their semi-final they had thrashed Grimsby 5-0. However, Tinn was a master when it came to pre-match psychology and, with his 'lucky' spats strapped to his ankles and comedian Albert Burden relaxing the players in the changing room before the game, the form book was turned upside down. Inspired by former Wanderers' winger Bert Barlow, who opened the scoring, the team romped to an historic 4-1 victory. Cliff Parker scored twice, wrapping up the win with a header, while 'Jock' Anderson scored the other.

Ironically, Pompey's League form had been dreadful. Four days after the semi-final the team crashed 2-8 at Middlesbrough and it took three successive wins in April to banish the threat of an unwanted 'double' – a Wembley appearance and relegation in the same season. The third of those victories, 2-1 over Grimsby, saw 18-year-old Portsmouth-born centre-half Reg Flewin make his First Division debut. Flewin had signed in November 1937 from Hampshire League side Ryde Sports and was destined to skipper Pompey to both championships. April 1939 also saw another small piece of the championship jigsaw fall into place when full-back Bill Hindmarsh swapped life in his native north-east for the south coast, signing from Northern League side Willington. The 19-year-old had already made his mark, playing in the 1939 FA Amateur Cup final at Roker Park, Sunderland. His team went down 0-3 in extra-time to Bishop Auckland.

With the books showing a healthy profit of more than £15,000, the club looked forward to the 1939-40 season with confidence, although inevitably the unfolding events in Europe meant that preseason training had about it an air of uncertainty. The heavy mood was hardly improved by the news in July that wing-half Jimmy

Guthrie had been seriously injured while driving his car in Yorkshire during an Air Raid Patrol (ARP) practice. This was ironic, as just two weeks beforehand, manager Tinn had decided to ban players from driving cars during the football season. Guthrie's life hung in the balance for a time, although he pulled through and was fit enough to return to action by December, as Tinn forgave his maverick skipper his breach of club discipline. Without Guthrie the team kicked off with a 2-1 home win over Blackburn on 26 August, but the air of impending war was underlined by the attendances at Pompey's two subsequent matches. Just 10,000 turned up at Derby in midweek to see a 2-0 win for the home side, while less than 13,000 were at Burnden Park, Bolton, the following Saturday, 2 September, just hours after German troops had invaded Poland. In normal circumstances those gates would have been three times bigger, but circumstances were far from normal. For the record, Bolton won 2-1 in what was to be Pompey's last Football League match for nearly seven years, but already minds were very much on other matters.

The following morning at 11am Prime Minister Neville Chamberlain announced to the nation on radio the declaration of war on Germany. All organised sport in the country ground to a halt. Touchingly, the FA entrusted Pompey with the safekeeping of the Cup, despite the fact that with its naval dockyard and numerous other military establishments Portsmouth would seem to be a prime target for enemy action. To this day, 'Portsmouth' is the answer to the question 'Which club has held the Cup for the longest period of time?' It was not until 1945 that the trophy was finally returned to Lancaster Gate. In a spirit of defiance, it was proudly displayed in the boardroom for every match during the war, even at the height of the Luftwaffe's blitz on the city during 1940 and 1941.

However, the Cup didn't always reside at Fratton Park. When the bombing was at its height it sometimes found a home in the vaults of the National Provincial Bank in Fratton Road, or was displayed in public houses around the area and even kept under the stairs at Jack Tinn's house. During one air raid, Richard Owen's grandfather, Albert Tupper, found himself sitting next to the Cup in the cellar of the Lord John Russell pub in Albert Road, Southsea, while its seemingly charmed life also allowed the trophy to survive being dropped and mislaid by player Bert Barlow. It took the skills of a Southsea silversmith – for a £120 fee – to knock out the dents and restore the club's pride and joy to its former glory.

Wartime football was a curious affair. The 1939-40 Football League season was suspended four days after the outbreak of war with just three rounds of fixtures completed. All professional contracts became null and void as the nation concentrated on the war effort. For almost two months no football was played at all, but by the end of October the FA had sanctioned two regional league and cup tournaments involving Football League members. Pompey returned to competitive action on 21 October, losing 1-2 at Fulham in a Regional League 'B' match. Football resumed at Fratton Park a week later with a 3-1 victory over Brentford in the same competition. The crowd was just 3,396. Grounds all over the country saw their capacities slashed – Fratton was limited to 8,000 – as the authorities fretted over the risks of concentrating large numbers of people in one place at one time, although it would be several months – following the so-called 'phoney war' – before the drone of German bombers would be heard over the Portsmouth skies.

Despite initial worries that professional sport might distract from the pressing task of preparing the country's armed forces for war, it soon became apparent that organised – if at times haphazardly arranged – football matches were in fact good for morale. However, as professional players volunteered for military service or received their call-up papers, the process of fielding a team was fraught with problems. Although clubs retained the registrations of their players, paying them on a match by match basis, military logistics saw many of them dispatched to the four corners of the land, or overseas. Pompey immediately lost the services of Guy Wharton, Freddie Worrall and Jimmy McAlinden from the team that played at Bolton. Wharton and Worrall would make the occasional outing for Pompey during the war years, but Irish international McAlinden would not return to Fratton Park until the resumption of the Division One programme in 1946.

Not surprisingly, players tended to guest for the club nearest to their barracks or station. One of the prime beneficiaries was the Third Division Hampshire backwater (in footballing terms at least) of Aldershot – home to the British Army. England centre-forward Tommy Lawton, not to mention the international half-back line of Cliff Britton, Stan Cullis and Joe Mercer, all wore the red and blue of the Shots. Indeed, in a 1-4 defeat at Fratton Park in November 1943, Aldershot fielded no less than six internationals, with Jimmy Hagan, Jim Cunliffe and Scot David McCulloch adding support to that England half-back line.

The flow of talent at Fratton Park worked both ways, for some of the great names of football guested for Pompey from time to time. After all, the city of Portsmouth was and remains the spiritual home of the Royal Navy. Arsenal's goalkeeper George Swindin and Welsh full-back Wally Barnes made single cameo appearances. The star of the show, however, was the Gunners' centre-forward, Ted Drake, who pepped up the Pompey attack on Boxing Day 1944, bagging four goals in the 9-1 demolition of Crystal Palace. The attendance, too, was swelled to over 13,000, restrictions on capacities having been relaxed after D-Day, once the threat of German invasion was finally banished.

On various occasions teams turned up short of players and had to 'borrow' from their opponents, or even the crowd – Brighton notably suffering when they travelled to Norwich one Christmas with just five players. Their scratch side eventually lost 0-18. Portsmouth, too, took advantage of a depleted Clapton Orient side at Fratton Park in February 1942 to record a 16-1 victory in which Scotland international forward Andy Black – registered with Heart of Midlothian – netted eight goals.

Pompey even managed a Wembley appearance, reaching the final of the London War Cup in May 1942, only to lose 0-2 to Brentford, a result perhaps partly explained by a pre-match row involving Pompey's abrasive skipper, Guthrie. A passionate defender of players' rights, Guthrie – who famously claimed he would have been paid more for playing the cornet than playing for Pompey in the 1939 final – used the high-profile occasion to raise the thorny issue of the club docking players' wages on the outbreak of war. Guthrie demanded that they be paid their arrears in full, or else the players wouldn't play. With kick-off approaching, the directors backed down and the showpiece game went ahead.

The attendance that day was 72,000, but that was hardly typical of wartime football. More often than not gates rarely made it into five figures. In November 1940 – with Portsmouth suffering badly from German bombing – just 803 paying spectators turned up at Fratton Park to see Bournemouth beaten 4-2. Two months previously the gate hadn't even been counted at the Goldstone Ground, Brighton, when enemy action forced an abandonment two minutes before half-time, with Pompey leading 2-1. In the spirit of the times, that Southern Regional League result was allowed to stand. The topsy-turvy nature of wartime football was probably never better illustrated than by two games between Pompey and Aldershot at the end of the 1940-41 season. On Saturday, 17 May at Fratton Park, Pompey trailed 1-3 at half-time in their Hampshire Cup semi-final, only to turn the game around in the second half to win by an improbable 10-5 after extra-time. Two weeks later at the Recreation Ground, Aldershot beat a virtually identical Pompey side 9-2 in a league match. Two days later, on 2 June, in their final match of the season, Pompey claimed the Hampshire Cup, beating Southampton 8-1 at Fratton Park.

Among the Pompey players who had enlisted in the Senior Service was reserve goalkeeper Ernie Butler, who had signed for the club in May 1938 from Bath City for a transfer fee of £100.

Butler spent three years at sea, returning home in 1942. His service commitments enabled him to guest for Bath and Tranmere, and the Birkenhead club attempted to sign him permanently at the end of the war. Their overtures were resisted and Butler went on to oust 1939 Cup final hero Harry Walker as first-team keeper during the 1946-47 season and become an ever-present in the championship years.

With his tall, slightly stooping frame and wavy hair, brushed back and centre-parted, the most noticeable features of this unassuming West Country lad were his huge hands, which time and again would come to Pompey's rescue in the post-war period to save seemingly certain goals. Donning the roll-neck green sweater, *de rigeur* for goalkeepers of the time, Butler would go on to give sterling service to Pompey in 240 League and Cup matches, until a broken wrist forced his retirement from the game in 1953. He eventually settled in Portsmouth, running, with his wife Evelyn, the George and Dragon public house in Fratton Road for many years, until his retirement.

Pompey's naval connection was strengthened as full-back Phil Rookes, who had signed from Bradford City in January 1938, joined the Royal Naval Volunteer Service and would see action on D-Day, while centre-forward Anderson – who would leave the club for Aldershot in 1946 – ended up packaging naval stores in the dockyard. Trainer Jimmy Stewart boxed artificial limbs for a naval surgeon, and Flewin helped to build army huts. Manager Tinn also assisted the war effort by packing footballs for the troops and organising a '20,000 sixpences' appeal to equip them with football gear.

The club also boasted their very own war hero in Cup-winning centre-half Tommy Rowe. Having joined the Royal Air Force when the war began, he was trained to fly Lancaster and Halifax bombers. Rowe's sorties over Europe severely curtailed his wartime playing career with the club. At one stage he was reported 'missing in action' before turning up safe and sound. He was awarded the Distinguished Flying Cross in December 1943, before being shot down in March 1944 over enemy territory and taken prisoner. By the end of the war Rowe was almost 34 and his playing career was over, but the Poole-born man, who had signed for Pompey from his hometown team back in 1934, had etched his name into the club's folklore.

This was the context in which Tinn commenced the process of building a Portsmouth team for peacetime – whenever that would be – and he was not slow to take advantage of the close links the Navy enjoyed with the club. However, arguably his most important signing was credited to the perseverance of Tyneside-born former

Pompey reserve Eddie Lever. Lever had joined the club as a 17-year-old, but with the club's blessing he had continued to train as a schoolteacher. Lever never appeared in Pompey's first team, signing for Aldershot, but a cartilage injury forced him to retire from playing in 1934. He took a job as a mathematics teacher at Alton, helping out with the coaching of the school team, and it was there that he first noticed the potential of a young lad called Jimmy Dickinson.

Naturally left-footed, Dickinson broke into Lever's youth club team on the left wing when aged just nine. That was no mean feat, considering the average age of the team was around thirteen. In Peter Jeffs' biography of Dickinson – *Pompey's Gentleman Jim* – Lever recalled that his protégé 'simply lapped up any tips I gave him'. Lever held Pompey in high regard – they had been particularly supportive of him when he had to retire, despite the fact he was playing for Aldershot – and he was happy to act as a part-time scout for the club.

In early 1942 Lever drove 16-year-old Dickinson to a Sunday morning trial at Portsmouth. By this time the boy had already played against the likes of Jimmy Hagan and Tommy Lawton in charity matches in Alton, but Tinn was not persuaded by what he saw, declining to follow up Lever's recommendation. Matters came to a head when Wolves wrote to Lever – who was by now virtually a surrogate father to Dickinson, following the death of his own father shortly after war broke out – seeking Jimmy's signature. Dickinson had impressed in a fundraising game against an Army team which included the Wanderers' full-back George Taylor. Taylor was not slow to relay to Molineux news of Dickinson's prowess.

Lever wrote back refusing permission outright, but also posted a letter to Tinn, conveying Wolves' interest and carrying the threat – although in fact it was more of a bluff – that Lever would encourage Dickinson to sign for the Midlands club. It did the trick, and on Saturday, 1 May 1943, Dickinson, now eighteen, made his Pompey wartime debut at left-half against Reading at Fratton Park in an end-of-season friendly.

Dickinson's signature was not a foregone conclusion, however, not least because he had a steady job at the Courage Brewery in Alton with good prospects, and in those days of the maximum wage a footballing career carried more risks than benefits. Nor was he a 'football fan', in the sense that Dickinson showed little interest in the professional game. Nevertheless he was flattered by the interest shown in him by Pompey, training with the club twice a week. In January 1944, a month after his full debut in the London War League, he signed professional forms.

Dickinson would complete his National Service in the Royal Navy – but not before a ten-month wait to join the RAF ended in rejection – and his appearances were limited in the 1944-45 season. However, it was in the October of that season that another couple of the championship jigsaw pieces began to fall into place. A match between the Royal Navy and a Royal Marines XI, featuring Flewin and Bill Pointon, left Pompey short of players for their own match with Watford. Local winger Peter Harris, eighteen years old, had just signed professionally. He was drafted into the side and shortly afterwards scored twice against the 'giants' of Aldershot. Meanwhile, starring in the Navy v Marines game was Jimmy Scoular, a sailor based at *HMS Dolphin* at Gosport, who had also turned out for the local team alongside Harris.

The youthful promise of Flewin hadn't escaped the notice of the international selectors either. He earned the first of two 'war caps' for England in September 1944 in the international with Wales at Liverpool which ended 2-2. His second appearance was in May 1945, with the war in Europe over. This time England beat Wales 3-2 at Cardiff. Dickinson was also rewarded for his progress, attracting attention while playing in an Air Training Corps international between England and Scotland at Clyde in April 1944.

In March 1944 the club had been delighted to announce that General Montgomery had accepted an invitation to become the club's President. 'Monty' had earned his reputation on the battlefields of North Africa, his Desert Rats defeating Rommel at El Alamein in 1942. Now one of the British Army's top brass, he was living in Portsmouth at Ravelin House. It was behind Portsdown Hill at Southwick House that he helped plan the D-Day landings of June 1944. One of Monty's first visits to Fratton Park in his official capacity came at the end of April 1944 to see the final League South match of the season against Brentford. To mark the occasion, the club put the FA Cup on public display and Tinn caused much amusement in the boardroom afterwards. Replying to Montgomery's query about where the club hid the famous trophy, Tinn replied, 'In football circles that is a closer guarded secret than that of the opening of the Second Front!' Monty would be a popular, if occasional, visitor to the ground after the war, frequently 'rallying the troops' via telegrams or letters to the team captain, Flewin.

Another quiet character in the dressing room, Reg Flewin led his future champions by example, with efficiency and discipline his trademark. Never the type to rant and rave – that was the preserve of trainer Jimmy Stewart – Flewin's physical presence on the field was accentuated by his exceedingly long neck. Upon it sat a head with a slightly receding mop of wavy brown hair, all of which combined to turn a man with a 5ft 10in frame into an apparent six-footer. He would go on to dominate the cream of First Division forward lines in the championship years, alongside his half-back colleagues Dickinson and Scoular.

By the turn of 1944-45 it was apparent that the war was drawing to its end and that the Allies would be victorious. Tinn – who in March 1944 celebrated his 25th year in management – set about preparing in earnest for the return to normality. Jack Froggatt, a 23-year-old inside-forward from Sheffield, signed as a professional in September 1945. He had first played for the reserves back in March 1941 and had made twenty first-team appearances during the war in which he scored six goals. Another player starting his career in the club's second string was the 20-year-old Jimmy Scoular, who first turned out against Aldershot reserves at Fratton Park in November. Scoular had been playing for Gosport Borough before he signed professionally for Pompey, which, as it turned out, would enable him to write a small, but interesting footnote in the history of the FA Cup.

Sunderland clear from Jack Froggatt. Centre-half Hall obscures Reid (Oct 1946)

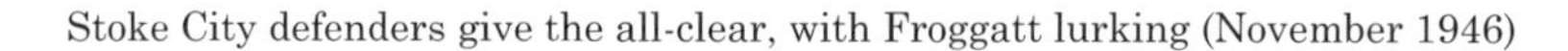

Stoke City defenders give the all-clear, with Froggatt lurking (November 1946)

Doug Reid scores past Charlton keeper Sam Bartram (November 1946)

Everton keeper Burnett saves from Fred Evans, with Reid looking on (Jan 1947)

Grimsby keeper Tweedy jumps for the ball with No 8 Doug Reid (March 1947)

Stoke keeper Herod is beaten by Cliff Parker's penalty (September 1947)

Stoke defenders pack their goalmouth to thwart Harris and Froggatt (Sept 1947)

Pompey outside-right Peter Harris misses the ball against Charlton (Sept 1947)

Burnley keeper Strong set to gather the ball ahead of the lurking Reid (Aug 1948)

Harris (No 7) scores past Blackburn's keeper Marks and No 3 Tomlinson (Oct 1947)

2

Return to Normal

1945 – 1948

With the war won, it was clear that the country at large – let alone Portsmouth, which had suffered disproportionately at the hands of the Luftwaffe – was determined to start enjoying itself again. War in Europe ended in May 1945 but the conflict in the Far East would continue for a further three months. With British servicemen still fighting and dying for their country, it was clearly neither practicable nor tasteful to reconstitute the league so quickly in its established format. However, in the summer of 1945 it was decided to run a regionalised – north and south – league competition reflecting the composition of the top two divisions as they had been in 1939-40. The Third Division clubs had their own similar competition. Football was far from 'back to normal' and getting a team out could still be fraught with difficulty. Take Pompey's regional League South fixture at Nottingham Forest in January 1946. Bill Shepherd, the driver of the Southdown Coaches team bus, came within minutes of making a shock debut after Guy Wharton, still in the Army based in the north-east, had failed to turn up. Jack Tinn ordered Shepherd – 'a thin, little man, what could have been going through his mind?' recalled Rookes – to get stripped and a pair of boots found, only for Wharton to turn up in the nick of time.

November 1945 also witnessed a tour of Britain by the footballers of Moscow Dynamo. The Soviet team stipulated fourteen conditions before undertaking the visit. These included taking all their meals in the Soviet Embassy and – as befitted the egalitarian nature of Soviet society – the split of all tour profits 50:50 between London and Moscow. The tourists attracted phenomenal crowds – 82,000 saw the 3-3 draw with Chelsea at Stamford Bridge. The other three matches ended with a 2-2 draw at Glasgow Rangers, a 10-1 thrashing of Cardiff and a 4-3 win over Arsenal at White Hart Lane. This final match elicited an official protest: at late notice the Gunners fielded a 'guest' player, Stanley Matthews, when one of their previously named team was unable to obtain a leave pass. This was contrary to one of the conditions laid down by the visitors. The match was also rendered farcical by fog, a situation which didn't help the Soviet referee, who insisted on both his linesmen running the same touchline, as was the custom in the Soviet Union.

It may have been impractical to resume league football in August 1945, but with the defeat of Japan that month it was not too late to get that season's FA Cup back on the rails. The Cup in those days carried greater kudos than the League and its return was keenly welcomed by the football public. But to spice up a depleted fixture list and sate the appetite of a war-weary populace eager for live professional sport, it was decided to play each round bar semi-finals and final on a two-leg, home and away basis. The Scot Scoular got his first taste of the competition in September 1945, playing for Gosport in a preliminary round. By the time Pompey entered the competition in the third round in January 1946 – competing at long last for a trophy they had protected for so long – Scoular had joined the club. Whether in innocence or out of mischief is not recorded, but Tinn fielded the technically 'cup-tied' and therefore ineligible right-half in the first leg of the tie at St Andrews. Birmingham City were on course for the Football League South title and won their home leg through Flewin's first-half own-goal. Perhaps the breach of rules was discovered, perhaps not, but either way Scoular was absent when Pompey failed to make up the deficit in the return at Fratton the following Wednesday. Pompey's hold on the Cup, measured in time as the longest ever, was, measured in rounds, as short as it could be. They had fallen at the first hurdle.

The nation's obsession with the FA Cup also contributed to the tragic events that unfolded at Burnden Park, Bolton, on 9 March 1946. It is estimated that some 85,000 crammed into the ground – despite an official attendance of 65,419 – to see Bolton reach the semi-finals at the expense of Stoke, Stanley Matthews and all. Stoke already led by two goals from the first leg. The unprecedented crush caused barriers at one corner of the ground to collapse, leaving 33 people dead and 400 injured. The subsequent Home Office report into the disaster recommended more rigorous licensing of grounds and the construction of smaller pockets of terracing.

In the League South, Pompey endured a miserable campaign, in a division which included the might of Arsenal and the minnows of Newport County, who had gained promotion to the Second Division back in May 1939. The Welsh team did the double over Pompey on successive Saturdays – 4-2 at Somerton Park and 3-2 at Fratton – as military demands wreaked havoc on attempts to field a consistent team. A final position of nineteenth out of 22 teams (there was no relegation, of course) hardly augured well for the reintroduction of a fresh First Division campaign, which was to start in August

1946. However, Tinn had used the season wisely, blooding the likes of Scoular and a 24-year-old London-born Royal Marine, who had taken part in the Normandy landings, called Len Phillips. He had signed in February after a successful trial spell and made his first-team debut at inside-forward in a 0-2 defeat at Wolves, a week after the second Newport defeat.

Tinn had capitalised on his scouting network in the lower leagues and in March, following a short 'guest' spell, signed a no-nonsense Scottish left-back named Harry Ferrier from Barnsley. Ferrier joined fellow Scot, inside-forward Duggie Reid, who had signed a fortnight earlier for £7,500 from Stockport. The close season also saw Tinn wield the axe. A number of old favourites – including 1939 heroes Lew Morgan, Tommy Rowe and Freddie Worrall – were handed free transfers. Guthrie, Bill Rochford and Anderson were all transfer-listed and soon moved on.

By the summer of 1946 the war in Europe had been over for more than a year but Britain was still ravaged by its effects. The optimism that followed the end of the conflict – epitomised by the Labour Party's overwhelming election triumph in July 1945, pledging to build a land fit for heroes – was ebbing away. Those heroes were slowly returning from far-flung corners of the globe to a land where the week-in, week-out grind of rationing was taking its toll. Not that professional football clubs were immune. As the new 1946-47 campaign approached, Pompey were forced to make a plea for 500 extra clothing coupons to ensure the team would start the season in pristine kit.

The Football League AGM in June 1946 had paved the way for 'normal' football to be resumed. To this end it was decided to replicate the divisional breakdown and the fixture list of 1939-40, irrespective of the fluctuation in club fortunes over the intervening period. Wartime giants like Aldershot found themselves back in the soccer basement, and Birmingham City, who in May had topped the Southern Division, eighteen places above Pompey, were in August back in Division Two, which had been their status in 1939. Little Newport, who had beaten Pompey twice in the first weeks of 1946, proved so bad in the Second Division that they would concede an astonishing 133 goals, thirteen of them in ninety minutes at Newcastle.

Such anomalies were inevitable, given the conditions of the time, but the restructuring introduced one bizarre consequence. No one could say for certain that in 1946 the teams in the First Division were better than those in the Second, and the process of natural selection would take several years to rectify itself. During the 1946-47 FA Cup, for example, First Division sides failed to exert their theoretical supremacy. Of the sixteen clubs to reach the fifth round, eight came from the First Division and eight from the Second, a split that continued all the way to the final. Some sceptics maintain that the effects of this disfigurement even diminished the two seasons in which Portsmouth were champions of England. In 1948-49, likewise, only half the sixteen clubs to reach round five came from Division One, and Second Division clubs reached Wembley in two of the first three finals after the League had been reinstated, 1947 and 1949. While it is true that in their championship years Pompey had to overcame the customary big-hitters – Manchester United, Arsenal, Liverpool, Wolves, Newcastle – what possibly remains in doubt is how good those teams were, relatively speaking, and how many Second Division sides were still the equal of those in the First.

However, it is churlish to carp at the subsequent achievements of the Portsmouth club. Second Division sides have performed well in the FA Cup at other periods too, notably the 1970s. Nor could the Football Leagues South and North in 1945-46 be regarded as an accurate barometer of relative footballing merit. Firstly, these were never designed as 'competitive' leagues, in the sense that promotion and relegation was at stake, and clubs would have approached matches safe in the knowledge their status was not under threat. In addition, professional players were still returning from their war service, disrupting teamsheets from one week to the next, and to have reorganised the divisions on the basis of these leagues – whatever Birmingham City's sense of grievance – would have created as many anomalies as it would have solved. Third Division clubs were excluded from the equation entirely, and Doncaster's subsequent record-breaking promotion would suggest they had merited a higher status in August 1946. Moreover, by the time Pompey were laying waste to all put before them, around a quarter of the teams in the top two divisions had swapped places. By 1949, those teams who might have laid claim to First Division status in 1946, yet found themselves in the Second, had either won promotion (and in the case of Manchester City and Birmingham been swiftly relegated again) or reverted to second class standards.

But this is to digress. The aforementioned AGM of June 1946 reported fourteen fresh applications for associate membership of the Football League, following rumours that it was intended to establish an extra, fourth division. They proved groundless and the closed-shop mentality of the 88 existing clubs (22 in each division) showed no signs of opening: the issue had only been raised because of a possible vacancy in the Third Division. In the event, New Brighton – who had not competed during the war years – were anxious to resume playing and did so. Should they have failed to complete their fixtures, the Football League evidently preferred the prospect of a 21-team Division Three (North), to that of admitting a League newcomer.

However, the principal debate involved minimum turnstile prices – currently 1 shilling 6 pence (8p) – for admission to League matches. The Chancellor of the Exchequer, Hugh Dalton, had recently rescheduled the taxation of football, reducing Entertainment Tax payable on turnstile income. He hoped to pass on some of this gain to the public. This was strongly resisted by Southampton, among others, who felt it would plunge clubs into a 'morass of debt', adding that the loss of income would compromise ground safety. After seven years neglect during the war, Southampton had a pressing need to bring their facilities up to date, and all clubs were bound to take heed of any recommendations made in the wake of the Bolton disaster. The Saints' pessimism, however, was not shared by the League Management Committee, whose proposal that 'some reasonable proportion' of standing accommodation be made available at 1s 3d (6p) was carried.

Other rule changes saw the maximum wage for players increased to £10 per week in the winter and £7 10s in the summer. Pre-war, these limits had been £8 and £6 respectively. Bolton Wanderers carried a resolution that no League ground should be used for greyhound racing, unless the practice was already established.

The first post-war Division One campaign started brightly for Pompey, with a 3-1 victory over Blackburn Rovers in front of 30,000 at Fratton. The team that day already included several key players who, two years on, would play their part in winning the championship. Rookes and Ferrier were paired as full-backs, while Dickinson made his First Division debut alongside Flewin. Harris started on the wing, supplying ammunition for Reid, who led the attack and scored two goals. Barlow, too, was in that line-up. In the next game, a 0-2 defeat at Derby, Froggatt made his Division One debut (scoring his first goal three weeks later in a 3-1 home win over Huddersfield). Pompey's third match was at Bolton, which they lost 0-1. This meant their start to the 1946-47 season mirrored that of 1939-40 – one home win and two away defeats against identical opposition. Football, it seemed, could be relied upon to bring a sense of symmetry to a world where most of the old reference points had been erased.

It was soon apparent that Pompey had little improved upon their dismal showing in the Southern Division just completed. Up to Christmas just five wins were earned and the team slumped into the relegation zone. Harris was quickly despatched to the reserves to learn his trade, while goalkeeper Walker paid the price for seven defeats in his first eleven games – in which he failed to keep a clean sheet. Come November Ernie Butler took over between the sticks – and stayed there.

It would get worse before it got better, and when Pompey travelled to Ewood Park for the return fixture with Blackburn Rovers on 28 December, they found themselves bottom of the table with just fifteen points. Drafted into the side that day for his debut was inside-left Len Phillips and, although he was only to make one more appearance that season, he proved to be the catalyst that sparked a run of six League wins and a draw. Also returning to the side was Scoular, whose Navy commitments had restricted him to just two appearances so far. He would be an ever-present for the rest of the season. It was at Blackburn that Butler kept only the team's second clean sheet of the campaign, and Froggatt's second-half goal earned a valuable win.

The only setback during that winning run was a single-goal fourth round FA Cup defeat at Birmingham, after Doncaster – who were running away with the Third Division (North) – had been overcome 3-2 at Belle Vue in the third round. Nevertheless, by the time Derby brought the 1946-47 curtain down at Fratton, winning 2-1, Pompey could look back on a mid-table twelfth place with 41 points from 42 games in an era when only two points were earned for a win. Ever-present Duggie Reid signed off the season with that solitary Pompey goal, taking him to 29 in the League, which equalled Jimmy Easson's feat back in 1931. The raw-boned, ungainly forward – not helped by his bow-legs – had more than won over an initially sceptical crowd with the ferocity of his shooting, hence his nickname Thunderboots. When he signed it was as a right-half, but it is believed trainer Jimmy Stewart recognised his potential as a forward and converted him. With his slicked down hair, parted on the left and craggy features, Reid's rangy, muscular body no doubt intimidated many a defender. However, the Scot's demeanour on and off the field was anything but fierce. Even when kicked up in the air, he would never retaliate, leaving the referee to administer any sanction as necessary, while in the changing room he was not one to use three words where one would do. However, he had a heart as big as an ox and his Pompey playing career would endure until he was nearly forty, at which point he served the club as groundsman until he retired in 1978.

That final game against Derby was played on Saturday, 31 May 1947 – the latest finish ever for a Pompey team – the season having been extended to take account of one of the severest winters on record. The situation was not helped by the Home Office ban on midweek matches, except by special dispensation, as part of the Government's 'National Emergency' measures to deal with the effects of the cold. Indeed, by the start of April Pompey had played just thirty League games and several clubs had to wait until June to complete their fixtures. The inclement weather also explains the attendance of just over 4,000 for Pompey's game at Huddersfield on the afternoon of Wednesday, 29 January. The game went ahead because the original fixture the previous Saturday had been postponed due to FA Cup commitments. For the record, a brace of goals from reserve centre-forward Fred Evans secured a 2-1 win in a raging blizzard to warm the cockles of the visiting dressing room. Phil Rookes also recalls feeling the wrath of Stewart at the interval after his poor headed clearance had allowed Peter Doherty to score for the Terriers on the stroke of half-time. 'Jimmy was a hard taskmaster and he certainly picked on me that afternoon! He was a Scotsman and boy could he swear. I'd been in the Navy for six years and heard nothing like it.'

To the astonishment of everyone connected with Portsmouth FC, the Derby match also marked the end of an era. Manager John 'Jack' Tinn announced his retirement before the game, after twenty years at the club. Having taken over the reins in June 1927 from Robert McCartney, the former South Shields manager had transformed the club into a First Division force, with a recent FA Cup pedigree bar none. Three Wembley finals had been contested in eleven seasons, not to mention another trip to the twin towers in 1942, and in 1936 his reserve side had the distinction of becoming the first provincial side to win the London Combination.

Tinn always had an eye for the theatrical gesture, such as his employing of a comedian – he was on friendly terms with radio and music hall stars of the day – in the dressing room before the 1939 Cup final, a move designed to diffuse any tension in his camp. His 'lucky' spats worn during that cup run was a typical psychological masterstroke and his players could always expect the unexpected. On the eve of Pompey's inaugural Division One campaign back in August 1927 he had organised a trip on a motor launch for fifty players and their families to Portchester Castle, quickly followed by a motor coach run to Hayling Island. On that occasion he missed the bus and had to catch up with the party by horse and carriage.

Although happy to leave the training to Jimmy Stewart, Tinn was widely regarded a 'player's man' and he inspired great loyalty among his charges. He was rarely seen in the dressing room, but fiercely protected his players from boardroom interference in team matters. So much so, it is said, that some directors were not too upset to see the back of him. Certainly goalkeeper Ernie Butler felt this was the case: 'When J W Tinn was in charge he would tell the directors what to do. I don't know if he was under contract at the time, but I reckon the Chairman Mr Stokes and Director Mr Wain got rid of him because they had no say in who was playing.'

To replace Tinn the club turned to a 'safe pair of hands' in the familiar and popular figure of Bob Jackson. The new manager had a penchant for bow-ties and had enjoyed a distinguished playing and coaching career at Bolton. He had managed Southern League Worcester City before joining Pompey before the war. Butler recalls 'The directors employed Jackson because he was chief scout, but in the end he was just lucky enough to take over Tinn's team. Although we saw him around the place, he was usually with the directors, not the lads. Jackson was more involved with the administration of contracts and the like, but Stewart was still the one who put us through our paces. On a match day Jackson would only put his head round the door of the dressing room to say "good luck",' concluded Butler.

A glance at the final 1946-47 League tables reveals how football clubs were struggling to come to terms with the ravages of war. The fixture list may have been identical to that of 1939, but there the similarity ended. It was estimated that around eighty professional players had lost their lives in action, while countless others – such as Guthrie and Walker at Pompey – had been robbed of their prime by the passage of time. Guthrie left Fratton in November 1946 to become player-coach at Crystal Palace, while Walker moved to Nottingham Forest five months later. This pattern of dislocation was repeated across the country and, as noted previously, in some cases clubs found themselves competing in what was patently the wrong division.

Never was this more apparent than at the bottom of Division One. Leeds United were relegated with a then all-time low eighteen points, having lost twenty of their 21 away fixtures, while Brentford, who joined Leeds in the drop, were clearly no longer the pre-war force they once were. At the top of the division, however, some familiar names had quickly reasserted themselves. Wolves – still managed by Major Buckley, finished third, beneath runners-up Manchester United on goal-average. One point ahead of them both, with 57, were Liverpool, who had emerged from pre-war mid-table obscurity to secure their first championship since 1923. But taking the geographical spread of the division as a whole, Pompey had at least one feather in their bonnet. The eleven teams that finished above them were all from the Midlands or the North. Even in such a mediocre season, Pompey were the leading southern club, finishing above Arsenal, Chelsea, Charlton and of course relegated Brentford – the only other southern clubs in what was a northern dominated First Division. Division Two, by contrast, had nine clubs south of Luton in its ranks. But as none of these were promoted, and Brentford had dropped down, the 1947-48 season would be even more geographically lop-sided than 1946-47.

Further evidence that the divisions had been inadvertently stirred, if not shaken up completely, could be found in the FA Cup. In the final, struggling Charlton Athletic retained the trophy they had lifted twelve months previously, beating Second Division Burnley 1-0. The Clarets had not only won promotion, they would finish third in Division One the following season, announcing their intentions at Fratton on the opening day, when they won 1-0.

The one unarguable fact about football in the immediate post-war era was that it exerted a huge appeal. Crowds flocked to games in unprecedented numbers. Pompey, on the back of 30,000 average home gates, made a profit of £20,000, while Burnley turned in a surplus of £17,000, as did champions Liverpool. In the summer of 1947 football's new-found prosperity was underlined when Derby upped the British transfer record, paying £15,500 for Greenock Morton forward Billy Steel. He was signed to replace Peter Doherty, who in moving to Huddersfield for £10,000 took his career aggregate of fees paid to £26,500. After much wrangling the players, too, saw some benefit from the increased revenues generated through the turnstiles. For 1947-48 the maximum wage was increased by another £2, to £12 in the winter and £10 in the close season. Bonus and talent money was accordingly improved, but burgeoning transfer fees were still causing unrest, as players were not entitled to a penny of the huge sums involved. In Italy – as noted by Ivan Sharpe in the *1947-48 Sunday Chronicle Football Annual* – players received thirty percent of their fee. British clubs resisted such moves on the grounds that it would give an 'obvious temptation to secure a change of club and a share of a fat fee'.

Increasingly, though, continental influences were permeating the British game. It was slowly dawning upon some far-seeing critics that our blinkered approach to playing the game would have to change if British teams were not to get left behind. The success of Moscow Dynamo's British tour in 1945 had been dismissed by some as a consequence of our teams still returning to full strength and fitness following the war. But what this implied about the state of football in the Soviet Union, which had suffered infinitely greater hardships than Britain, was hard to imagine. Instead, a 6-1 drubbing handed out by Great Britain to the Rest of Europe in a representative match at Hampden Park in May 1947 reinforced the imperious attitude that all was well. Wiser voices, perhaps, pointed to the fact that Swedish club Norkopping had also embarked on an unbeaten British tour, embarrassing their various hosts with some astute positional play. But Phil Rookes insists other factors had to be taken into account: 'Sweden had not taken part in World War II, so had the benefit of excellent conditions, food and the good things in life. It must have benefited their players.'

Not that Pompey were unduly concerned about such matters. The 1947-48 season started well, despite early hiccups against Burnley and Stoke. Four successive wins at the end of September – among them a 6-0 thrashing of Sheffield United at Fratton – put the club among the early pace-setters. The squad built by Tinn was maturing fast, but new manager Jackson quickly realised that a centre-forward was a top priority if the potential of the team was to be realised. Jackson's role was to be evolutionary, rather than revolutionary, although he showed he was not afraid to take hard decisions, selling 1939 Cup hero Jimmy McAlinden to Stoke for £7,000 shortly after the start of the season. That particular decision would return to haunt the club. Jackson also made an audacious bid of £17,000 for Chelsea and England's Tommy Lawton, but the deal foundered on the London club's insistence that Jimmy Dickinson sign for them as part payment. Dickinson was going nowhere.

However, in November 1947, as a run of four defeats in five matches toppled the team back into mid-table, Jackson finally got his man. Tipton-born Ike Clarke was a Black Country lad, and with his 33rd birthday just two months away he could hardly be regarded as in his prime. But these were different times. The war had ravaged the best playing years of many, but it also prolonged the careers of others and gave opportunities to some who might otherwise have missed out. Clarke's eye for goal was not in question. In 37 Second Division matches for West Bromwich Albion the previous season he had netted twenty times. So, for a fraction of the price Lawton would have commanded, the 'last link in the chain that would carry Pompey to the pinnacle had been forged', according to Mike Neasom in his book *Pompey: The History of Portsmouth Football Club* (1984).

With his dark hair brushed back without a parting, Clarke was undoubtedly an intelligent footballer who more than made up for his fading pace with some astute positional play and exceptional timing. He also lacked his front teeth, as many centre forwards did (and do), and he would wrap up his dentures and put them in his locker before going on to the field. He was well-built, but preferred to use his brain rather than his brawn, most notably in the 5-0 thrashing of Newcastle in the first championship season. According to Rookes, he 'hardly touched the ball', but managed to draw the Magpies' centre-half Frank Brennan out of position, enabling wingers Harris and Froggatt to snap up five headed goals. 'It was a brilliant display,' recalled Rookes.

Clarke scored on his debut – a 2-4 home defeat by Aston Villa – but despite being first choice throughout January and February he added just four more to his tally. One of those came in the 4-1 home demolition of Brighton in the third round of the FA Cup. In the following round a 1-3 home defeat by Preston left the team with little to play for in the coming months. It is not recorded whether or not Jackson was unhappy with Clarke's initial impression, but in March the board sanctioned the outlay of a further £10,500 on Dundee's 28-year-old former Huddersfield Town centre-forward Albert Juliussen.

It was to prove a curious signing all round. Juliussen had made his post-war reputation leading the Den's Park outfit to promotion from Division 'B' north of the border in a team that scored 113 goals during 1946-47. In Pompey's 6-1 home win over Middlesbrough in early April Juliussen completed a hat-trick, then scored in a 2-0 win at Everton, giving him four goals in seven games. However, for the last match of the season, at home to Chelsea, Clarke was reinstated, scored the winner and never looked back. Juliussen never again pulled on a first-team shirt and Pompey recouped their investment when selling him to Everton in August 1948. Rookes recalls: 'The training was just too much for Albert and he wanted out! After his first morning's training he said to me "I won't be here long" and he was right!' Len Phillips, too, recalled the conversation, but was slightly less charitable: 'He wasn't a bad player, but he had the pace of a carthorse. You have got to have pace if you are playing up front.'

With the 1947-48 season completed, Pompey experienced at first hand that the English game had much to learn and that the 'continentals' could no longer be regarded as a soft touch. The club embarked on a five-match tour of Scandinavia, winning just one – 2-1 against AIK Stockholm – and losing three times, once to the famed Norkopping. Although the results were a dent to collective pride, Jackson could look back with satisfaction on a first season in charge, which had seen the team finish in eighth place with 45 points from 42 games. That position had been largely built on the strength of a sound record at Fratton Park – just three defeats all season. Indeed, after Manchester United claimed both points with a 3-1 win on 27 December, Pompey won seven and drew two of their remaining nine home matches. Championship form, no less. And Chairman R Vernon Stokes knew it. With the club's Golden Jubilee almost upon it, his rallying message to the troops for the eve of the following season was all but written.

Doug Reid heads Pompey's first goal against Grimsby (November 1947)

Man Utd keeper Crompton tips Harris's shot over the bar. Pompey wear red socks (Dec 1947)

Stockport keeper Bowles smothers the ball at the feet of Ike Clarke (January 1949)

Baldwin, Brighton's keeper, is grounded as Guy Wharton's goal levels the scores (Jan 1948)

Wharton and Reid watch as a Bolton defender clears off the line (January 1948)

Sunderland's keeper is deceived by Peter Harris's shot in this 2-2 draw (April 1948)

Believe it or not Harris's effort hits the bar with Sunderland's defence nowhere (April 1948)

Pompey team picture at Villa Park (September 1949)

Reid challenges Middlesbrough keeper Ugolini for this high ball (September 1948)

Sheffield United goalie Smith climbs higher than Len Phillips (September 1948)

3

Golden Days

July – November 1948

Richard Vernon Stokes, a Portsmouth solicitor, had taken over the chairmanship of the club from Stephen Cribb in September 1946. Stokes' message to the team on the eve of the 1948-49 season was short and to the point: win the Championship for the Jubilee! 'The directors are looking for the team to make it a real year of history. Portsmouth are largely off the football map, and nobody thinks of Portsmouth as champions. People always think of Arsenal or Manchester United as teams from which the champions come, but not Portsmouth. It is obvious, though, that if we are to achieve our ambitions as a club this season we must keep our eye on the ball for the whole ninety minutes of every game and play with an enthusiasm which would be appreciated by the club officials and the very loyal band of supporters,' he added for good measure.

Portsmouth Football Club was celebrating its fiftieth birthday season, having been formed on 5 April 1898, when a group of local businessmen and sportsmen met at 12 High Street, Old Portsmouth and agreed to buy five acres of agricultural land close to Goldsmith Avenue. Their desire was to create a top-class football team for the city, having cast envious glances along the coast to Southampton, where the St Mary's club had gone from strength to strength since its formation in 1885 and admission to the Southern League.

The city's top club at the time was the Royal Artillery, who had reached the FA Amateur Cup final in 1896 only to lose to Bishop Auckland by a single goal. In 1898-99, as the fledgling Portsmouth club was building its stadium and acquiring the players and management necessary for a successful application to the Southern League, the RA reached the final again. However, in retreating to the east coast for a week to prepare for the match against Harwich, with the players incurring 'expenses' – for cigars and brandy no less – they were deemed by the FA to have breached the strict 'amateur' rules and found themselves suspended. Stockton took their place in the final, taking the trophy 1-0 and the RA disbanded as a football club shortly afterwards, leaving the way clear for the new club to establish itself.

The foresight and ambition of those founding fathers of the club – John Brickwood, Alfred Bone, John Peters, William Wiggington, George Oliver and John Pink – was now, half a century on, about to be fulfilled at the highest level. The group of players Jack Tinn had assembled were being carefully nurtured by Bob Jackson, who, to be fair, as chief scout, had played a significant role in spotting and attracting Tinn's signings to the club. Pre-season training in those days was a far cry from the modern trend of training camps, foreign tours, fitness coaches, special diets and weight-monitoring, adopted by the top, and not so top, clubs today.

Ernie Butler recalled how the players reported back for training after the summer break around six weeks before the first match of the season. This usually meant the first or second week in July, depending on the fixture list, which was typically published, then as now, in late June. The first month of pre-season training would see the players reporting to Fratton Park for a morning and an afternoon session. 'We would spend the first two weeks basically lapping the perimeter track of the pitch to get our fitness levels up, then the next fortnight we would do a mixture of lapping and sprinting and also some ball practice.

'In the final two weeks of training we would ease down and only report for the 2-4pm afternoon session on a Tuesday and Thursday, which nine times out of ten would involve a walk down to Southsea seafront from where we would disperse. At least twice a week as well, during the run up to the season, we went to Milton Park for a session of bowling, designed for relaxation and recreation.' As preparations were stepped up for each new season, after half an hour's sprinting the ball work would largely involve practice matches on the Fratton turf, featuring the first-team forwards against the first-team defenders.

'The matches,' Butler continued, 'under the eye of Jimmy Stewart would last for about an hour. Even when we played public practice matches it tended to be the first-team attack and reserve-team defence against the reserve-team attack and the first-team defence, although things might be changed at half-time to give some people experience.' As a goalkeeper, a few concessions were made in Butler's training routine: for example, he remembered doing more sprinting than lapping, but facilities for doing much else were limited. 'I used to practice throwing a ball against a wall and catching it, but to be honest I don't think any other clubs were much different in the approach.'

Pre-season training in the summer of 1948 culminated with a couple of public practice matches in which the 'Blues' – that is to say the probable first team – met the 'Reds', the likely reserves. The Blues duly took the first match 3-2 with Harris netting twice and the other coming from Juliussen in front of a crowd of 6,400. The only notable absentee was full-back Yeuell, who had picked up a heel injury in training. For the final trial Clarke led the Blues' forward line in place of Juliussen, who was the subject of increasing speculation about his future at Fratton Park. Certainly 'Ranger' – the football correspondent for the *Evening News* and *Football Mail* – was in no doubt. Echoing Rookes' and Phillips' earlier assessment of Juliussen's prowess, he wrote in his review of the Blues' 3-0 win in front of 7,134: 'He is far below 100 percent fit and until he recovers much of it we cannot hope to see him in the League side.' Even when Clarke cried off with a mouth abscess on the eve of the opening game, manager Jackson chose to switch Froggatt to centre-forward and bring in Barlow on the wing, rather than turn to his expensive spring signing.

In spite of the chairman's bold challenge, on the evidence of these two games there was little to suggest that either players or supporters really believed that this could be their season. The 1947-48 title had gone to Arsenal, who had seen off the challenge of FA Cup-winners Manchester United by a seven-point margin. Their meeting at Manchester City's Maine Road – Old Trafford was in the process of being renovated after bomb damage – in January 1948 had also underlined the phenomenal popularity of the game in this period, as 81,962 crammed into the stadium to see a 1-1 draw. During the summer of 1948, as the all-conquering Australian cricketers humiliated England, with skipper Don Bradman averaging 89 runs an innings, the smart money was on one or other of these giants making the running again. Arsenal were underpinned by their wing-halves, Joe Mercer and Archie Macaulay, and possessed a forward line as potent as most, led by Ronnie Rooke, who scored 67 goals in 88 League appearances for the Gunners before moving to Crystal Palace. United had also finished runners up in 1947 and – despite Arsenal's prominence – were widely regarded as the best footballing side in the country. Their left-winger, Charlie Mitten, was blessed with a terrific left foot, while England international centre-forward John Rowley could be relied upon to bag a goal every other game.

In any case, no team south of London had ever won the championship, and Portsmouth – despite their Cup successes – were regarded largely with indifference by the London press, who doted on the mighty Arsenal. The Pompey team had no internationals in their line-up, were in the hands of a diligent but uncharismatic manager, and were unfashionable in every sense of the word. Which made their unbeaten start to the new campaign all the more incredible, although the run almost ended before it began in the opening game at a drizzly Deepdale against Preston North End.

Before the match the portents were good, as the party made the long coach journey north. Pompey hadn't lost at Deepdale since 1925, but now they trailed 0-2 with less than half an hour to go. A typically mazy Tom Finney dribble and cross had set up the opener for half-back Willie Dougall to score on the stroke of half-time. Soon after the break the Preston 'plumber' – these were the days when footballers needed a trade behind them as insurance against injury and retirement – scored a penalty when Jimmy Scoular up-ended him in the area. Once Duggie Reid headed home Jack Froggatt's cross, however, the tables were turned and 1939 Cup hero Bert Barlow came up trumps with the equaliser. On the same afternoon it is curious to note football's increasingly global appeal, as a team from India – for the most part playing in bare feet – saw off an Isthmian League XI 3-1.

From the foundations of this resilient, rather than exuberant performance at Deepdale, Pompey proceeded to sweep all before them. The sun was out at Fratton Park for the following Saturday's game against Burnley and Froggatt's header secured the second two points of the week (it would not be until 1981 that three points were awarded for a win) – Everton having been fortunate to escape with a 4-0 beating on the Wednesday. Everton's defiant goalkeeper that evening, Ted Sagar, was injured for the return seven days later at Goodison Park as Pompey went to the top of the table, winning 5-0 in front of more than 41,000. Such was their dominance that Butler in the Portsmouth goal didn't touch the ball until an hour had passed. On 4 September 1948 Pompey retained top spot thanks to a flattering single-goal win at Stoke City, on a day on which all the club's teams – first, reserves and youth – were unbeaten. Pompey had spent the week based at Blackpool and the Everton game provided the opportunity for the transfer of misfit forward Albert Juliussen to the Toffees to be finalised. Pompey recouped the £10,500 they had paid Dundee back in March and the sale was confirmed on the morning of the Stoke match. Meanwhile, at Fratton Park, more than 11,500 turned up to see Pompey reserves fight out a 0-0 draw with neighbours Southampton.

The following Saturday Middlesbrough descended on Fratton and although the Teessiders showed considerable spirit, having lost 1-6 at Preston last time out, there was no denying Pompey. With three minutes to go, Jimmy Dickinson started a move which was finished in typical fashion by the boot of Duggie Reid. It was now around eight hours since Pompey had conceded a goal. Mr E Dryer, a South Stand season ticket holder living in Haslemere Road, writing in his scrapbook, recalled that 'Middlesbrough goal-keeper [Ugolini] kicked the ball away with disgust and temper and it bounced once and went behind the Portsmouth goal, where

Rookes retrieved it.' Pompey's defensive shut-out lasted another 61 minutes in the next game at Fratton against Charlton, when wing-half Benny Fenton – who would go on to manage Millwall – scored their consolation in a 1-3 defeat. That win lifted Pompey three points clear of Wolves at the top. Despite the good start there were still rumblings from 'Ranger' that the team's attack was not up to the standard required to sustain a title challenge. It would be a familiar refrain over the next two years.

Pompey's avowed policy was to develop players of their own rather than pay inflated transfer fees, and having almost got their fingers burned with the expensive signing of Juliussen, the board were reluctant to rush into another big-money deal. Instead, the club's network of scouts up and down the country busily kept tabs on the lower leagues, looking for promising hopefuls who could be transformed into First Division players. At one board meeting in August 1948, no fewer than fourteen reports on players of this type were tabled. Pompey were also keen to recruit local talent, with the latest a 17-year-old grammar-schoolboy and inside-forward, John Beale, who had signed professional forms in the summer and learned this month he had earned honours in Latin, French, English and history in his Higher Schools Certificate. According to Rookes, Beale would customarily complete the *Daily Telegraph* crossword during the fifteen minutes between arriving at the ground and starting training!

The club had also developed an excellent network of contacts in Scotland, highlighted by the fact that chairman Stokes and director Syd Leverett were the only representatives from the English game invited to the AGM of the Scottish Central League in Ayr. The esteem in which the club was held north of the border was enhanced by the surprise presentation to the league by Mr Stokes of a trophy to be known as 'The Portsmouth Cup', to be competed for by its member clubs. Back in England, however, the club was facing allegations that their players were 'dirty'. A Football League official specifically went to see Pompey play at Manchester City on 18 September but could find nothing wrong. 'They are just a strong robust side that keeps pegging away for ninety minutes and that's what gets them home,' he reported. Other teams who had played Pompey, notably Middlesbrough and Everton, were also quick to spring to their defence.

It was back to the functional rather than the brilliant as the team eked out both points in the return at Middlesbrough, then again at Manchester City. In both games Pompey had to recover from the shock of conceding an early goal. The match at Maine Road also saw the rare spectacle of a clutch of Pompey fans up in the stand, having braved the tortuous overnight coach journey –

remember the first motorway in England didn't open until 1959 – from the south coast. Those doughty few would have entertained the growing conviction that this could be the club's year. The following week, as Pompey entertained Sheffield United, the South Stand – built in 1925 to one of architect Archibald Leitch's typical designs, with a steel lattice-work front – was declared full at 1.30pm. By kick-off, 36,000 were in the ground to see Pompey secure a 3-0 win. Around that time the club trimmed its playing staff, transferring reserve left-half John Foxton and centre-half George Hudson to Third Division (South) Swindon.

It was the following Saturday, 2 October, that provided the first acid test for this team without stars, which was now threatening to usurp the traditional football power bases of London, the north-west and the north-east. Newcastle United were in town, just two points behind Pompey in second place, newly promoted from Division Two and intent on restoring the club to its pre-war eminence. It must be said that most of that glory predated World War I, but four championships and seven FA Cup final appearances still made the Magpies a major attraction.

No one should doubt that Portsmouth were a well-supported club – even compared with their First Division counterparts – and gates of 30,000 were the norm. Those gates mostly comprised home supporters, although Pompey could always rely on a significant Naval contingent, up to 5,000 or so – the sailors clearly identifiable on the terraces in the sparkling white caps of their uniform. Some sailors of course would support their own home-town club – should they be facing Pompey. It was also customary for sailors to support the opposition whenever they found themselves spectators at another ground. That said, Pompey were the Navy's 'team' and most of the *matelots* who found their way down Goldsmith Avenue on a Saturday afternoon would be found cheering the Blues. Portsmouth's isolated geographical location, in the days when car travel was a luxury and coach travel slow and uncomfortable, meant that large numbers of visiting supporters – save for FA Cup-ties and when Arsenal were in town – were rare at Fratton. For this match against Newcastle, the *Football Mail* reported that there were just eight Geordies who had made the 330-mile journey through the night to follow their team.

Queues at the turnstiles, which normally opened around 1pm, on what was to prove an unseasonably warm autumn afternoon, started forming by late morning. The gates were closed at 2.50pm with 45,827 inside – 1,800 or so short of the ground record, but the biggest League gate of the season – and several thousands locked out. As the combination of the heat and the crush took its toll, the St John Ambulance brigade was kept busy reviving fainting fans.

Ground capacities were fairly arbitrary in those days. The football annuals of the day reckoned Fratton Park could hold 60,000 – although this figure was never remotely tested – and despite the tragedy at Burnden Park just a couple of years earlier the safety of the fans was largely reliant on a posse of 'crowd packers'. This now extinct occupation involved inspecting the North Terrace from the perimeter of the pitch to ensure an even spread of fans and avoid over-crowding.

One supporter at the time, John Danagher from Copnor, who as a child saw his first match in 1947, remembers their role distinctly. 'I would go to the match with three or four friends and I can recall sometimes being physically passed down over the top of the crowd to the front. The gangways of the terrace were numbered from 1-15 and the stewards would use loud hailers to direct people to where there was space. As I recall, it cost 9d (4p) for us boys to get in and when Pompey ran out in those days they always went to the Milton End, or 'Boilermaker's Hump' as it was called, after the dockyard craftsmen who stood there.'

Mike Barnard, who lived in Alverstone Road, which runs parallel to the Milton End of the ground, taps a similar vein. 'The one thing I remember was the crowd. Each gangway had a numbered circular board on a pole and the crowd would be directed with a loud-hailer to where there was a spot. The ground was always full of sailors in their white caps, and in those days Pompey were known as the Royals. I also remember how virtually everyone seemed to come to the ground by bicycle. When the dockyard workers came out they would ride up to the ground and people living around Fratton Park would take in the bikes and look after them in their sheds and front rooms for a few pennies.'

The match against Newcastle ebbed and flowed, without ever living up to its top of the table billing. Late in the first half Newcastle felt they should have been awarded a penalty when full-back Phil Rookes seemed to handle in the box, only for the referee to wave aside their appeals. The luck was with Newcastle, however, as Reid missed a sitter from close range. Reid was to atone in the 65th minute when his pass set up Len Phillips, who held off a challenge before firing home the only goal. Londoner Phillips was one of those for whom the war almost cost him a career in professional football and it was only Pompey's military scouting network that had noticed his talents while playing for the Royal Marines. A beautifully balanced player and adept with either foot, his wiry frame always kept defenders potentially on the wrong foot. With his slicked down hair, parted on the left, he perfectly complemented the intelligent forward play of Clarke. He was largely a lover of home life – he particularly resented the way matches at Christmas would impinge on his time at home – and mostly kept himself to himself, unless the subject turned to his main passion: football and its tactics. To this day he still loves discussing the intricacies of the game and confesses that he prefers to watch the more technical Italian game to English football. He is rarely seen at Fratton Park nowadays, although he still lives in the city, but his wife Joan remains a season ticket holder.

By this time preparations for celebrating the club's jubilee were well underway, with a special meeting of shareholders authorising a £2,000 outlay for the event in November. Chairman Stokes proposed that two representatives from each League club be invited to a special function on 29 November, as well as officials from the Football Association, Football League and representatives from clubs in Ireland and Scotland. But in the meantime, Pompey had matches to play.

Having seen off Newcastle the team travelled the following Saturday to take on Aston Villa. The interest generated by Pompey's start was indicated by the fact that dozens of coaches had been hired to ferry supporters to the game. There was a healthy contingent from the south coast at Villa Park, sporting their blue and white rosettes, and their presence helped swell the gate to more than 57,000. One supporter who made the journey was Mr Dryer, who recalled in his journal: 'I travelled to Birmingham to see this match, leaving Portsmouth at 6am. We stopped at Abingdon for breakfast and then met bad fog at Stratford-on-Avon. We left Birmingham at 7.30pm and stopped at Woodstock from 9pm-10pm and again met fog as far as Winchester, arriving home at 1.20am on Sunday.'

Villa were struggling at that time and should have been beaten. Reid put Pompey ahead, rounding the goalkeeper in the 66th minute. He might have scored beforehand, but the referee ruled Froggatt had crossed from behind the goal-line for his header. Mr Dryer had no doubt that goal should have been allowed: 'We had stand seats on a level with the penalty area at this end of the ground and the ball was centred by Froggatt before it went over the line. Aston players did not appeal and were returning to the centre when the referee suddenly changed his decision and awarded a goal-kick.' Ambrose Mulraney equalised with a fierce shot from the edge of the penalty area. That match saw its share of injuries. Pompey trainer Stewart wrenched a knee running onto the pitch to attend to a player, and twelfth man Jasper Yeuell had to take over his duties, while Villa's 'Sailor' Brown broke a jaw in a collision with Ernie Butler. Mr Dryer was not in the mood for sympathy: 'Thousands of Portsmouth fans travelled to this match, which was spoiled by the exceedingly rough play of Aston Villa, with Brown the chief culprit and Dorsett not being at all fussy about his methods. The Aston crowd seemed to appreciate this sort of thing. Portsmouth did well to get a point out of such a murderous game.' Stewart's injury was covered by the short-term appointment as trainer of former Crewe boss Frank 'Tiger' Wood.

Driving rain slashed the attendance for the next Saturday game against Sunderland at Fratton, meaning the 'full house' signs could be stowed away for once. The Rokerites' captain, Fred Hall, arrived at the ground with the curious record of not having lost a toss for nine consecutive matches. He should have known it wasn't going to be his day when referee Pearce's coin fell in Flewin's favour. So it proved, as Pompey cruised to a 3-0 victory, despite Barlow having a goal disallowed and Froggatt being forced to limp off after a heavy tackle, reducing his team to ten men. It was to be another seventeen years before substitutes would become part and parcel of the English football scene.

With the undefeated run now extending to thirteen matches, the question was how long it could continue. Pompey's next outing was at Molineux to meet a Wolverhampton Wanderers team uncharacteristically marooned in mid-table. The Midlands side had established themselves as one of the strongest in the country under Major Buckley's military-style management just before the war. They had been League runners-up in 1938 and 1939 – not forgetting their losing Cup final appearance against Pompey – and they had quickly reasserted themselves upon the resumption of peacetime football. Third place in 1947 had been followed by fifth place in 1948, but with England international keeper Bert Williams between the sticks and England captain Billy Wright at centre-half, Wolves' potential still appeared unfulfilled.

Before kick-off, chairman Vernon Stokes read out a letter from club president Monty – now Field Marshall Lord Montgomery of Alamein – congratulating them on the start to the season. However, the players failed to take their cue and Wolves raced into a two-goal half-time lead. Billy Wright smashed home a thirty-yard free-kick, then Butler made an uncharacteristic error, letting John Hancocks' shot slip from his grasp and over the line. Pompey came out fighting after the interval, but controversy stalked their efforts as Reid fired home, only for Wolves to protest furiously that he was offside. After consulting with his linesman, Mr Blythe concurred, and when Phillips's shot came back off the inside of the post it clearly wasn't going to be Pompey's day. Sammy Smyth, Wolves' Irish international winger, wrapped up the two points with a deflected shot.

Pompey looked suddenly vulnerable as October came to an end. Bolton became the first side to take a point from Fratton, holding out for a 0-0 draw, with manager Jackson away in Scotland spying on a player. Derby County, who had emerged as the chief threat, knocked Pompey off of the top of the table on goal-average (goals scored, divided by goals conceded, a system which was replaced by goal-difference in the 1970s) with a 2-1 win over Chelsea. During that week, Portsmouth FC announced a profit of £12,361, less taxes, on the previous financial year and work was completed on a flat piece of terracing at the back of the Milton End, designed to ease access for supporters.

The following week Derby consolidated their position as Pompey displayed a lack of killer instinct against mid-table opponents. Twelfth-placed Liverpool benefited from some profligate finishing, enabling them to run out 3-1 winners on 6 November. Seven days later thirteenth-placed Blackpool came within four minutes of winning at Fratton. Aside from two appearances by reserve centre-half Gerry Bowler (signed from Northern Ireland side Distillery in August 1946) – who replaced the injured skipper Flewin – manager Jackson had been able to name an unchanged team for sixteen consecutive matches. However, for the visit of Blackpool – who with Stanley Matthews in their team swelled the gate to over 44,000 – he felt it appropriate to ring the changes. In came centre-forward Ike Clarke for his first start of the season, in place of Bert Barlow. The inside-forward hadn't scored since September, although he had twanged the Anfield bar the previous week. Clarke was joined, intriguingly, by a debut-making Jamaican inside-forward called Lloyd 'Lindy' Delapenha, who took the place of the injured Len Phillips.

Former soldier Delapenha earned the distinction of becoming Pompey's first black footballer, at a time when in England it was still rare to see a black face in society at large. Having played Army football in the Middle East, he had joined the club in April 1948, after failing to make an impression at Arsenal as an amateur. 'Olympian', who followed the fortunes of Pompey reserves for the *Football Mail*, was initially sceptical about how this 'colonial' would settle down with the other players. 'In the succeeding months I have noticed that he is just "one of the boys". His team-mates have accepted him as a matter of course and they all indulge in the normal joking and leg-pulling with one another,' he was relieved to find! Despite Jackson's attempts to shake things up, Pompey continued to labour up front against Blackpool and with six minutes remaining their worst fears appeared to be confirmed. Referee Green from Wolverhampton had been in a picky mood all afternoon, penalising foul throws left, right and centre, but when Rookes challenged Blackpool's Dumfries-born centre-forward Jimmy McIntosh in the penalty area there seemed little doubt that he had won the ball cleanly. Mr Green disagreed, awarded a penalty-kick, and Stan Mortensen sent Butler the wrong way. Pompey's unbeaten home record looked lost, but they rallied immediately, Harris cutting in from the wing in typical fashion to level. After the game Delapenha was delighted with the experience. 'I enjoyed every minute of it. The speed of the game had me worried for a time, but when I get used to it I'm sure I'll be fine. If only that first-half shot of mine had scored I would have been the proudest player in the world,' he told a reporter afterwards. And when news filtered through that leaders Derby – the following week's opponents at the Baseball Ground – had lost 0-3 at Newcastle and were therefore just two points better off at the top of the table, Pompey's situation looked even brighter.

Derby were, in many ways, a similar club to Wolves. Although they had yet to win a League championship – that honour would have to wait for the Brian Clough-Peter Taylor partnership in 1972 – in the immediate pre-war years they had established a reputation for being there, or thereabouts, at the top end of Division One. They had won the FA Cup in 1946 and in 1947-48 finished fourth in the League. Nor were they a club averse to splashing out in the transfer market. Their inside-forward Billy Steel remained the most expensive player in the game during the 1948-49 season, but in this particular match it was his partner, centre-forward Jack Stamps, who ensured Derby went four points clear. He had already hit a post in the first half, when, shortly after the interval, Butler lost Stamps' cross-shot in the sinking sun. Pompey's paucity of goals in the League was rubbed in by the fact the reserve team thrashed Aldershot 7-0 at Fratton Park that same afternoon in front of a crowd of more than 6,000. Off the field, Trainer Stewart's injury meant he could no longer run properly, so a reshuffle saw Jimmy Easson promoted to first-team coach, with Stewart re-designated 'supervising trainer'.

Back in the summer Pompey had designated their home game against Arsenal as their Golden Jubilee match and the Football League arranged for the fixture to be staged on 27 November 1948. However, few could have believed four months previously that it would also present a vital clash between two pretenders to the First Division title. The choice of Arsenal was a natural one. They were, simply, the biggest club in the land, regularly attracting crowds of 60,000 to their marbled halls of Highbury. They were also the reigning champions of England – as they had been five times in the 1930s under the management of the legendary Herbert Chapman – and had been largely responsible for shifting the balance of power in English football from the north down to London. Although they had yet to rediscover the rhythm that had taken them to the title, Arsenal were handily placed in fourth position and had yet to concede more than two goals in any game during the campaign.

Arsenal also had a reputation for being 'lucky' – a tag that stemmed from the fact that they had 'talked' their way into the First Division when it expanded in 1920, despite finishing seventh in Division Two. But it would have taken all their luck and more to deny Pompey on this afternoon. Supporters had started queuing at 2.40am – Mr H Atkinson of Catisfield, near Fareham claimed that honour – and there were around 150 outside the ground at 9.15am waiting for the gates to open at 11am, reported the *Evening News*. Under the gaze of Montgomery, present for the occasion, a giant birthday cake cut in the boardroom with the help of FA Secretary Stanley Rous, was iced by the events of the match itself. Within twelve minutes Arsenal's defensive credibility had been shattered by Froggatt's snap effort and Clarke's shot on the turn. Nine minutes after the interval Phillips latched onto a loose back-pass to make it 3-0. Scoular then fouled Botley-born ex-Saint Don Roper and Reg Lewis converted Arsenal's spot-kick. However, the final word – appropriately enough considering a phalanx of former heroes had paraded before the game – belonged to Bert Barlow, the sole 1939 Cup-winner still in the team, who converted Clarke's cross.

'I have never seen a team come on the pitch so determined to win as Portsmouth did today and they gave the finest exhibition of football I have ever seen and in the end the Arsenal players could hardly raise a trot so thoroughly beaten were they,' concluded a contemporary match report. 'Ranger' concurred in Monday's *Evening News*, claiming it was Pompey's best performance since their Cup final win. Although the Arsenal team had been invited to attend the jubilee celebrations that evening at the Savoy Ballroom, they were on a train home within an hour. Tails firmly between their legs, no doubt.

Another curious absentee from the club's jubilee dinner at the Savoy in Southsea the following Tuesday was former manager Jack Tinn, who had done more than most to create this winning side. Instead, he had to content himself with a pint at his local, the Royal Anchor in Liphook, where he lived. His omission was highlighted in a special *Picture Post* feature on the club and its celebrations. Reporter David Mitchell summed up the irony: 'Yet, when Portsmouth, at the height of its jubilation, welcomed its old players and football personalities from all over Britain, Jack Tinn was not invited – the man who, for so long, in the eyes of the world *was* Portsmouth. Perhaps his greatest achievement (winning the 1939 Cup final) was also his unforgivable fault. The new football era is an era of directors and the days of the all-powerful manager are past ... to celebrate the jubilee without Tinn was to exclude one of the most effective high priests, or at least one of the subtlest witch doctors, that soccer has ever known.'

Portsmouth were destined to climb heights even Tinn couldn't have envisaged, but to exclude from their jubilee celebrations the man who had guided Pompey to their only major success – the 1939 FA Cup – left a sour taste.

Newcastle keeper Fairbrother spectacularly saves Froggatt's header (Oct 1948)

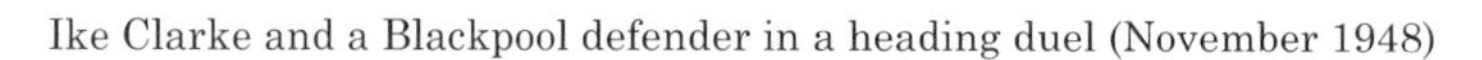

Ike Clarke and a Blackpool defender in a heading duel (November 1948)

A typical pose from the great Jimmy Dickinson

George Farm, Blackpool's goalie, saves during a Pompey attack (Nov 1948)

J W Tinn

Harris creates a goal in Pompey's Golden Jubilee match with Arsenal (Nov 1948)

Stanley Rous (FA Secretary) helps skipper Flewin cut Jubilee cake (Nov 1948)

Crompton, Man Utd's goalie, saves this effort from Ike Clarke (December 1948)

Chelsea goalie Pickering catches, watched by Clarke and Froggatt (Dec 1948)

Herod, Stoke's keeper, takes a high ball under the gaze of Ike Clarke (Jan 1949)

4

Winter of Content

December 1948 – February 1949

And so the jubilee glory went to Pompey, but more importantly it renewed self-belief in a team which had been in danger of losing its way. If the mighty Arsenal could be overturned so comprehensively, there was no team left in the League for Pompey to fear. The impact on collective belief in the team's ability to win the championship was dramatic, although it wouldn't be until the New Year that performances truly began to reflect Pompey's patent superiority.

The week following the win over the Gunners, Pompey travelled to lowly Huddersfield, with speculation rife in the press that Reid – left out two weeks previously against Blackpool to rest his injured leg – was the target for a number of clubs, notably Arsenal, who were looking to boost their attack. The Gunners were particularly keen to recruit someone before the 25 December deadline, for this would make any new capture eligible for the third round of the FA Cup. 'Ranger' reported that Reid might not be averse to a move to Highbury.

Huddersfield – fresh from a 4-2 win at Newcastle – were finding it hard to live up to their pre-war eminence. During the 1920s they had been managed by Herbert Chapman, latterly of Arsenal fame, and had themselves been League champions – three years in succession in the mid-1920s – not to mention being runners-up twice. They were now in their 29th consecutive season in the top flight, but it was clear they were living on the edge. They had finished twentieth in 1947, nineteenth in 1948, and would end up twentieth again this time. But in an age when only two clubs were relegated they were still somehow clinging to safety.

In a bid to bolster their fading fortunes, in December 1946 they had paid one of the biggest transfer fees of the period, £10,000, to sign Northern Ireland international centre-forward Peter Doherty. Although at 35 he was past his prime, he remained a potent threat and would continue bagging goals at a rate of one every other game in the lower divisions with Doncaster right up to his fortieth birthday. Now, on this grim West Yorkshire afternoon, he came closest to breaking the deadlock before half-time but his lob just cleared the bar. Pompey – in their change colours of red shirts and black shorts – should have fallen behind early in the second half when Jim Glazzard missed from four yards. Phillips might have nicked an undeserved winner near the end, but the goalless draw meant that Derby, 5-0 winners over Charlton at the Baseball Ground, were able to re-establish a three-point lead at the top of the table.

The following week Middlesbrough tabled a bid for Duggie Reid, but the Portsmouth board said no, seeking a forward in exchange rather than a straight cash deal, while another Lancashire club also made an enquiry. At the same board meeting Vernon Stokes was re-elected chairman.

Pompey were unchanged for the home draw with fourth-placed Manchester United, dropping a point in the last five minutes when United wing-half Bill McGlenn headed home. Although Pompey had trailed to Charlie Mitten's first-half penalty, two goals in three minutes by Froggatt and Clarke seemed to have enabled the home team to extend their advantage over United from three points to five. It is also strange to note that the Fratton Park crowd dipped below 30,000 for only the second time that season. Although the Manchester club were regarded as one of the most entertaining in the country, they had yet to earn the cachet of, say, Arsenal, or even a Matthews-inspired Blackpool.

The gate was even lower for the final fixture before Christmas, the return match with opening-day opponents Preston North End, but this weekend in the football calendar had long since established a reputation for poor attendances. In December 1935 less than 8,000 saw Pompey win 2-1 at Grimsby on 'Black Saturday' and twelve months before that fewer than 10,000 had turned out for the First Division match between Leicester and Portsmouth. Before the war it was rare for this particular weekend's gate to exceed 20,000 at Fratton Park, so in the circumstances a crowd of more than 26,000 was cause for satisfaction, reflecting not only the success of Pompey, but also the post-war boom generally in Football League attendances. Those paying customers would have returned home delighted, too, as the two clubs' respective fortunes had diverged dramatically since they fought out a 2-2 draw back in August. While Pompey had established themselves as genuine title contenders, Preston found themselves in twentieth place and were headed for the drop.

Like Huddersfield, the Lilywhites had enjoyed pre-war success, winning the FA Cup in 1938, 1-0 against West Brom, thanks to a last-minute penalty. However, the Preston legend had been built back in the formative years of the Football League. The club had won the inaugural championship in 1889, plus the FA Cup, to give them the 'double', an achievement that in more modern times would become a Holy Grail for clubs seeking to prove they were the cream of the crop. Since those heady days of the late nineteenth century, Preston had become something of a yo-yo club, and the string was currently on the downward track.

The gate that afternoon might have been higher had Preston been able to include England winger Tom Finney, but injury had ruled him out of contention. Pompey's 3-1 victory put them back into second place, just a point behind Newcastle, going into the Christmas fixtures.

Christmas Day 1948 proved to be gift-laden for Portsmouth FC. Having won 2-1 at Stamford Bridge against Chelsea, a game in which the Pensioners' Scottish international inside-forward Tom Walker made his final League appearance, Pompey players waited for other results to filter through on the BBC's wireless service. The wireless brought good news. Pompey had been the only team in the top five to win and were back on top of the First Division for the first time since October. It was an advantage they were determined not to let slip.

As was the long-established custom in the Football League, opponents squared up twice over Christmas. Chelsea thereby provided the Boxing Day opposition at Fratton Park, where more than 43,000 saw Pompey complete the double, though rather less convincingly than the 5-2 scoreline might have indicated. It was only when Chelsea full-back Danny Winter sliced into his own net that the points were secured, with Barlow's penalty two minutes later giving the scoreline a flattering edge. Chelsea's goals came from centre-forward Roy Bentley, who was fast establishing a reputation which would earn him a call-up for England's 1950 World Cup campaign. Star of the two victories was undoubtedly Peter Harris, and manager Bob Jackson was moved to comment afterwards: 'There is only one Stanley Matthews, of course, but Harris will get a cap yet I'm certain.'

Although Harris would go on to represent his country, there is little doubt the two caps he earned were a poor reward for his talent. Portsmouth born and bred, and with a slightly unruly parting which would flop over his forehead even in the most formal of pictures, Harris was the 'babe' of the championship team, having just turned 23 in December 1948. His slender frame – 'there was nothing to him at all', recalled Phil Rookes – no doubt helped him cultivate a turn of pace which would leave full-backs trailing in his wake. This was coupled with the ability to use a sway of the hips which left defenders on the deck, making him a potent weapon in the Pompey armoury. Not only did he score more than his share of goals for a winger (208 in all competitions during a fifteen-year career at Fratton), he also was an unselfish player – reflecting his slight diffidence perhaps – who would invariably tee the ball up for a team-mate if they were better placed.

After basing themselves in Blackpool for a couple of days, Pompey's momentum was briefly disrupted at a snowy Turf Moor on New Year's Day. It was a rare outing on the first day of the year for Pompey, as, unlike Scotland, which had always featured a full holiday programme of fixtures, England would not adopt the New Year as a bank holiday until 1974. In 1949, 1 January fell on a Saturday, however, and for Pompey it brought a daunting fixture. Their three pre-war League visits to Burnley had brought three defeats, in which Pompey had scored once and conceded ten goals. The Clarets were re-establishing themselves among the elite after a seven-year absence. They had reached the FA Cup final in 1947 and finished third in the First Division the following year. With snow and sleet making conditions slippery underfoot, their new signing from Preston, Andy McLaren, converted a cross from Harry Potts – who would in time be a successful manager of Burnley – to win the match 2-1.

Remarkably, Pompey had used only fourteen players during the season so far, and Jackson was able to announce an unchanged team for the following Saturday's FA Cup third round home tie against Third Division (North) outfit Stockport County. When the draw had been made Jackson had opined 'It suits us'. One player disappointed not to be in the team was Reid, who had signed from Stockport in 1946. With the incumbent forward trio of Barlow, Clarke and Phillips linking well, however, the Scot had to content himself with reserve football, while rumours continued to circulate about his impending transfer. The FA Cup has been traditionally regarded as a good leveller, but not on this day, as Peter Harris helped himself to a hat-trick and Clarke and Phillips a pair apiece to record a 7-0 win in front of more than 33,000 supporters. The match was also a first for trainer Billy Wright, who had joined the Pompey staff on 3 January.

The team's reward was another home tie in the fourth round against Second Division Sheffield Wednesday. It was also learned that neighbours Southampton, chasing promotion to the First Division for the first time, had been anxious to sign veteran winger Cliff Parker, but the Portsmouth board refused their overtures. Two new players arrived at Fratton – young Scottish full-back Alex Wilson, who would serve the club with distinction for many years, and 21-year-old ex-Wolves winger Ron Bennett, about to be demobbed from the RAF.

Jackson was forced to change his team for the meeting with Stoke City at Fratton on 15 January, as full-back Phil Rookes had injured an ankle the previous week. He was replaced by 23-year-old Bilston-born Jasper Yeuell, who had played as an amateur at West Brom before signing professionally for Pompey in August 1946 when he left the Army. Pompey shrugged off the effects of the change, however, despite the referee missing a first-half penalty, when not one, but two Stoke players handled the ball. Froggatt's cross deceived the goalkeeper to give Pompey the points.

The team were establishing a reputation for a tight defence and rapid counter-attacking. These tactics – to the extent that the word 'tactics' could ever be said to apply to the English game in the late 1940s – stood them in good stead at Charlton for their 27th match of the season. The direct railway line from Portsmouth to London encouraged several thousand Pompey fans to swell the gate to an astonishing 61,475. They witnessed win number fifteen, secured via Clarke's fierce shot, which Charlton goalkeeper Sam Bartram couldn't hold. Newcastle's draw at Stoke meant Pompey were now three points clear of the Magpies at the top.

Attention once again turned to the FA Cup. Sheffield Wednesday's Cup pedigree was built upon three previous triumphs, the most recent in 1935. This particular tie also threw up a direct confrontation between Sheffield-born members of the footballing family Froggatt. Jack, at 26, had established himself as a key member of Pompey's line-up on the left wing, while his cousin Redfearn – two years younger – was a barnstorming centre-forward who would score more than 130 League goals for the Owls in fourteen seasons' service. Both would gain full international honours for their country.

That Cup 'exclusive' was eclipsed that day by the exploits of Southern League Yeovil Town, who wrote themselves into FA Cup folklore by beating First Division Sunderland 2-1, having already accounted for Second Division Bury in the previous round. By comparison, Pompey's 2-1 win over Wednesday was small beer. Any chance of a shock was quickly snuffed out when Harris levelled three minutes after Eddie Quigley's opener. With both teams playing in their change colours, Pompey in red and the Owls in white – as the rules of the competition dictated when a clash occurred – Phillips secured the victory in front of a 47,188 crowd, which was fewer than 500 short of the ground record.

That record gate had been set for the FA Cup fifth round tie with West Ham in 1939, and its survival had less than three weeks to run. The draw for the fifth round on Monday lunchtime paired Pompey with either struggling rivals Huddersfield or Third Division (South) Newport County. For the first time, the prospect of Portsmouth being the first club in modern times to complete the 'double' began to dawn. Monty, in typical fashion, sent a telegram from Switzerland to the team before the home League fixture with

Manchester City. He urged them to 'concentrate on the League as it takes a good all-round team to win that', hitting a different note to many supporters, who felt that the glory of the FA Cup was still paramount.

Such, for example, was the view of Betty Rowse, who lived just around the corner from the ground in Bramshott Road during the championship years. She had been taken to her first match by her uncle during the 1937-38 season and still remembers getting into trouble with her parents – who ran the Dukes Head public house in Lucknow Street – for not arriving home until late one night in April 1939. Her crime was to have gone to see the Pompey team return to the Portsmouth Town (known as Portsmouth and Southsea today) railway station with the Cup. She recalls: 'In the championship years the team was so good that the supporters took it for granted. They were wonderful years for going over to Fratton Park and I feel sorry for some of the younger supporters who missed all that, but for me winning the FA Cup in 1939 was far more of an achievement than winning the League.'

Spurred on by fervent support in the second half, as the famous Pompey Chimes echoed round the ground, the team recovered from a goal deficit at half-time to beat City. Once Clarke had equalised with an overhead kick with twenty minutes to go, Pompey took charge and rewarded their chiming hordes with two further goals. Harris exhibited his poaching instincts as a goalscoring winger without peer, then Clarke added a third. The origins of the Pompey Chimes – 'Play Up Pompey, Pompey Play Up' – are derived from the hourly chime of the Guildhall clock. It is reported they were first heard in the ground in the early 1900s, and they have since become synonymous with the club. Although they were, and still are, regularly heard throughout games, in the late 1940s they were particularly associated with Pompey launching an attack. And their sound reverberated way beyond the confines of the stadium. 'Everyone sang them in the ground,' recounted Betty, 'and my mother used to tell me she could hear them at the pub, which was over a mile away, when the wind was in the right direction.' The chant would be given a new arrangement – specially composed by Major Vivian Dunn, Director of Music, Portsmouth Division, Royal Marines – which was aired for the first time in the forthcoming FA Cup fifth round tie against Newport. Incorporating the 'Chimes' into a song, Major Dunn's version was also recorded as a 78 rpm (revolutions per minute, in the now obsolete gramophone age) vinyl disc and sold in local record shops, but it never really caught on with the public.

Although the Chimes were the pre-eminent Pompey chant of the day, they were augmented by shouts of 'Come on you Royals!'

However, the penchant of one particular individual in the Fratton End, or Station End, as it was referred to in the *Football Mail*, sticks in the mind of several contemporary fans. 'There was always a sailor in the Fratton End who would yell out "Set 'em alight",' recalled Betty. Her recollection is shared by John Danagher, who also remembers the sailor calling out: 'Come along my lovelies!' John Phillips, a promising schoolboy footballer at the time, who would later play for Pompey, also remembers a cough-sweet seller patrolling the edge of the pitch. 'He would yell "Cough no more!" at the top of his voice. Customers would throw coins down at him and he would throw the sweets back.'

The club's long-standing love affair with the FA Cup was seemingly about to write another chapter, but before the anticipated glory of the Quarter-Final there was the little obstacle of Newport in the fifth round to overcome. The Welsh club's fortunes had nose-dived since their appearance alongside the likes of Arsenal, Pompey and Chelsea in the Football League South in 1945-46, and their subsequent relegation from the Second Division a year later. If any club had good reason to curse the intrusion of the war it was Newport. As champions of the Third Division (South) in 1939, they never had the chance to consolidate in the higher sphere, and found themselves totally unprepared for its demands once the war ended, having to pull together the frayed threads of their professional squad.

The Ironsides arrived at Fratton Park just three off the bottom of the Third Division (South). Although they would rally, they were locked into a cycle that would see them apply six times for re-election to the League, until the Third and Fourth Divisions were created in the reorganisation of 1958. However, 12 February 1949 saw arguably one of the Welsh club's finest moments. They had already eliminated Second Division Leeds, then First Division Huddersfield in a replay. On their arrival home from Yorkshire hordes of County fans mobbed the players, causing club officials to fear for their safety. Newport's heroics encouraged thousands of their supporters to embark on the train, and for the unfortunates, a tortuous coach journey, to Portsmouth. Their presence helped Fratton Park set a new ground record of 48,581. Though Phillips gave Pompey an early lead, the match was quickly transformed. First Bob Harper, then Eddie Carr, scored for Newport from close range.

When Phillips capitalised on goalkeeper Alex Grant's bad positioning to level ten minutes into the second half, few doubted that Pompey's class would finally prevail. Would it heck. County still looked the more likely winners as the match went into extra-time. In those days, the rules of the FA Cup gave clubs the option of taking the first match into an extra thirty minutes, provided they both agreed beforehand and informed the referee of their decision. This seems strange, considering the loss of revenue and kudos from staging a replay. After all, Newport lost out on the chance of packing Somerton Park and possibly beating Portsmouth in the process. Whatever the reasons, it was a decision Newport would rue. Had County's Len Comley not muffed a golden chance from close range early in the extra period to make a name for himself it might not have mattered. However, a replay still looked likely as Barlow scorned the chance to settle it from the penalty spot. But Newport keeper Grant smothered his shot, awarded for Ray Wilcox's handball. With five minutes to go Froggatt finally settled the tie when he fired home after a goalmouth scramble. And so it was that Portsmouth's number went into the hat for Monday's draw and, as in 1939, it came out lucky once more, giving the team a fourth consecutive home tie, this time against title rivals Derby. For supporters brought up on the talismanic powers of J W Tinn's spats, Wembley Way was looming larger than ever in their thoughts.

The only cloud on the FA Cup horizon was the intractable problem of satisfying the demand for South Stand tickets, which at that time provided the only seating at Fratton Park – the upper section of the North side being terraced. Time and again the club was forced to respond to complaints in the *Evening News* from aggrieved supporters who had missed out on the precious piece of paper entitling them to entry to the match. As a result, the club's decision to issue – without warning – vouchers at the Manchester City game on 5 February, entitling holders to priority for future all-ticket Cup-ties, had been widely welcomed. The club had also been approached with a plan to seat the upper tier of the North Stand, but the directors ruled this out in the short term, as it would substantially reduce covered accommodation for standing supporters. However, the directors announced their intention to increase the seating capacity in the 'next two to three years'.

One of the curious facets of Pompey's rise to prominence is the absence of capped players on their books. Aside from the wartime recognition afforded to Flewin, the England international selectors had apparently bypassed the south coast. In those days the selection process for the England team was by committee. The England team did not have a manager in the modern sense of the word – who could pick and choose his teams – until Alf Ramsey in 1963. His predecessor, Walter Winterbottom, was beholden to men in suits who did the job for him.

Indeed, the chairman of the selection committee, Arthur Drewry, was in the stands at Bramall Lane to survey these south-coast upstarts as they sought to consolidate their position at the top of the Football League. The game looked one sided on paper, as Sheffield United, who would end up bottom of the division, had just been knocked out of the Cup, 0-3 at Wolves. When Barlow scored after just two minutes – 'Ranger' was keen to admit his error in crediting the goal to Froggatt in Saturday's *Football Mail* – the omens looked bleak for the Blades, but Pompey never really got going and wing-half Harry Hitchen soon levelled. At half-time Flewin needed treatment for a cut eye, which delayed his reappearance for the second half. In those pre-substitute days the trainer had no option but to patch him up as best he could, but by the time Flewin was back on the field United were ahead and went on to win 3-1. Drewry was obviously unimpressed by these southern impostors. When the England squad was announced for the Scotland match on 9 April, Portsmouth players were conspicuous by their absence. But it would not be long before such oversights were rectified.

Len Phillips' effort is touched over by Sheffield Wednesday's McIntosh (Jan 1949)

Flewin (No 5) shakes hands with Wednesday skipper Quigley (January 1949)

Flewin leads out red-shirted Pompey against Sheffield Wednesday (Jan 1949)

Peter Harris heads in a corner past Wednesday keeper Westlake (January 1949)

Jack Froggatt (No 11) challenges Wednesday's goalie for this high ball (Jan 1949)

Pompey raid the Manchester City goal in a game they won 3-1 (February 1949)

Newport's Harper (No 11) levels at 1-1 in an epic-cup-tie (February 1949)

Newport keeper Grant punches clear from Clarke (No 9) and Phillips (Feb 1949)

Butler saves v Derby. This game breaks Fratton's attendance record (Feb 1949)

Peter Harris and Aston Villa full-back Cummings chase the ball (March 1949)

5

At the Double

February 1949 – May 1949

Cup-fever for the looming quarter-final with Derby was such that it soon became apparent that the ground record would be under threat again. Going into the match, manager Jackson was able to recall Peter Harris, who had missed the defeat at Sheffield United through injury. Making way for him was 1939 Cup veteran Cliff Parker, who had signed for the club back in December 1933 from Doncaster Rovers, and who at 35 still had much to offer Pompey as a reliable stand-in winger.

It was generally accepted that to obtain a good vantage point at Fratton Park on a match-day it was necessary to arrive by 1pm. On Saturday, 26 February 1949, however, the queues for the turnstiles began forming soon after breakfast time. At 2pm the gates were shut with a never-to-be-bettered record crowd of 51,385 jammed into the ground. They had paid record receipts of £5,465. Enough to cover the wage-bill for several weeks in those days when players earned just £10-£12 per week.

Cyril Lucas, from Gosport, was working as a builder at the time and attended that Derby cup-tie. 'My friends and I had a usual Saturday routine where we would wander down to Gosport town centre around 12pm and catch the ferry to Portsmouth. We were down there a bit earlier on this day though! The ferries were usually packed on a match-day and were a bit smaller than they are now and the fare was about 3d (2p). When we got to The Hard on the other side we would go and get something to eat and then catch a bus up to the ground. There were dozens of Corporation buses heading to Fratton Park, at a fare of 2d, but there was also the choice of a Byngs coach to the ground which cost 6d. The buses came and went like trains and it appeared just like a conveyor belt moving people to the game.

'We always stood opposite the tunnel on the North Terrace and on the day of the Derby cup-tie we were packed in like sardines. When we arrived, Frogmore Road, which leads down to the main entrance, was absolutely full. We were standing shoulder to shoulder and it was impossible to lift your arms up. There was always a band at the ground, either the Fire Brigade or the Royal Marines, and you needed something to entertain you as nothing much happened beforehand, except for perhaps the opposition coming out to look at the pitch in their suits.'

When the match started, it was soon clear it was going to be a classic. Derby lay third in the First Division, and back in November they had inflicted a 1-0 defeat on their hosts at the Baseball Ground. They had spent the week preparing at Hindhead, thirty miles or so up the A3 between London and Portsmouth, and the change of scenery seemed to have done them some good early on as they dominated the opening exchanges. First blood went to the Rams when, in the 41st minute, Reg Harrison's corner was headed home by centre-forward Jack Stamps. But within three minutes Ike Clarke had replied with a booming header from Jack Froggatt's centre. The second half ebbed and flowed. At one point it seemed Derby's former England international winger Frank Broome was bound to score. He found himself with the goal at his mercy but Ernie Butler was able to smother his weak shot. Almost at once Clarke raced to the other end and a swing of his left boot looked to have put his side in the semi-finals. There was still time for Broome to save his blushes, but in the last minute he sliced a shot so wide it nearly hit the corner flag. Speaking to *Daily Express* reporter Frank Butler afterwards, Clarke relived his winning goal: 'Froggatt took a quick throw-in to Phillips who lobbed the ball high into the area. I nodded the ball down to my feet, trapped it and cracked it in before the goalkeeper knew much about it. I think Leuty [the Derby centre-half who was marking Clarke] was deceived into thinking I was heading the ball goalwards.'

'Afterwards it was pandemonium,' recalled Cyril Lucas. 'All the crowd wanted to see Ike and I remember he couldn't come out to speak to anyone because he was eating a sandwich! Eventually, because there were so many people milling around outside he had to leave the ground by a back entrance. When Pompey won you were elated and we would walk back to the ferry replaying the game in our minds. However, if Pompey lost I was depressed until Wednesday.'

The spring in supporters' steps soon had extra bounce when the draw for the semi-final pitched together the big boys of Wolves and Manchester United, leaving Pompey the best of all options, a tie against Second Division Leicester City to be played at Highbury. Tickets for the game were like gold-dust, but it was still more than three weeks away and in the meantime there was the League title to concentrate minds. Aston Villa were beaten 3-0 at Fratton Park, despite arriving in good form which had seen them pull clear of the relegation zone. The following Saturday a reshuffled forward line – Froggatt moved to centre-forward to replace the injured Clarke, with Parker coming in on the left and Duggie Reid returning in place of Bert Barlow – had too much class for Sunderland at Roker Park. Reid was soon back in the groove with a pair of goals in a 4-1 win. That match also underlined the close affinity between the club and the Royal Navy, with a coachload of supporters having driven overnight from Rosyth Dockyard, near Edinburgh, to cheer on their favourites. The match coincided with director Harry Wain's birthday and 'Ranger' recalled that Wain bought champagne for everyone in the party before they left Newcastle at 10.30pm to take the sleeper train back to London. In those days the reporter for the local newspaper tended to travel with the team and understandably built up close ties with people at the club. At times 'Ranger's' review of the week in the *Football Mail* tended to reflect more the views of the club establishment, rather than the gripes of the supporters, but at others he would offer trenchant comment on matches if he felt the team wasn't performing to scratch.

Transfer deadline day came and went with a flurry of activity, Derby splashing out a world record £24,000 on Manchester United forward Johnny Morris. Bob Jackson contented himself by beating Manchester City to the punch to sign promising 23-year-old inside-forward Reg Pickett from non-league Weymouth. Derby paraded Morris in their return to Fratton three weeks after their Cup disappointment, being desperately keen to revive their flagging title hopes. However, in front of another huge crowd, Len Phillips' first-half goal sealed a 1-0 win. With ten games to go Pompey were now five points clear at the top. It looked like boiling down to a two-horse race with Newcastle United, who Pompey were due to visit a couple of weeks later.

Beforehand came the semi-final with Leicester City. The two sides had met at the same stage of the competition in 1934, Pompey winning 4-1 at Birmingham City's St Andrews ground, and confidence was high that a similar result could be achieved. At one point, queues for tickets stretched from the main office at the end of Frogmore Road all the way to Alverstone Road, nearly half a mile away. Fans anticipating a canter into the final and a chance to repeat the glory of ten years earlier quickly snapped up Pompey's 23,000 allocation. British Rail put on sixteen special trains to carry supporters to London, with a return ticket costing 12s 6d (63p). June Veal, now living in Cornwall, was thirteen at the time and recalls cycling from her home in North End to Fratton Park during the middle of the night to secure her place in the queue. 'Afterwards I had my photo in the *Evening News* taken with a group of other fans madly waving our precious pieces of paper. It never occurred to any of us that Pompey would do anything other than win. After all, we were the top dogs' she added. Her confidence was mirrored by Mrs Joan Phillips, wife of Len, who travelled up on the train with other players' wives from Portsmouth. 'We were wearing our rosettes on the Underground to Highbury when we met some Leicester supporters. They were all convinced they were going to lose and were just hoping they played a good game,' she recalls.

Opponents Leicester couldn't quite make up their minds which division they belonged in. Since their election to Division Two in 1894 they had regularly jumped up a division then fallen back, all without ever winning a major trophy. The closest they had come was in the First Division in 1929 when they were runners-up by a point to Sheffield Wednesday – the same season in which they had inflicted Pompey's record defeat, 10-0 at Filbert Street. Legend has it that ten swans flew over the stadium that day. However, since City's relegation from the First Division in 1939 their fortunes had waned. They entered this match with the prospect of Third Division football a distinct possibility for the first time.

In the Cup, though, Leicester were made of sterner stuff. In the third round they had put out First Division Birmingham after two replays, and had trumped that by beating another top division side, Preston, 2-0 at Filbert Street. In the fifth round they prevailed 5-3 at Luton Town in a replay, before another Second Division side, Brentford, were dumped at home in the quarter-finals. Leicester's pivotal player was 21-year-old centre-forward Don Revie, who was in the process of transforming the revolutionary art of the deep-lying centre-forward.

In the late 1940s, whatever the fancy-dan continentals were up to, British football was essentially a simple game in which tactics or coaching played little part. Players lined up from the goalkeeper in a strict 2-3-5 formation, with each position allocated a role, which rarely changed from club to club. The two full-backs' job was to mark the opposing winger and cover the centre-half if play was on the opposite side. A full-back would rarely venture over the halfway line, unless the game was being chased. The centre-half would mark the centre-forward, supported by his left and right half-backs, who had a broadly defensive role to fill. Wingers would remain on the touchlines, waiting for the inside-forward to come deep, receive the ball and project passes in their direction. The winger's task was then either to dribble past the full-back or use his speed to latch onto a deeper pass. Converting the resulting crosses was the responsibility of the centre-forward, his inside-forwards pushing up in support. It is no coincidence that in the 1948-49 season all but two of Pompey's goals were scored by forwards. The other two were own-goals.

With this in mind, some fans theorise that Revie's clever play, which would earn him two goals that afternoon in Leicester's shock

3-1 win (and England caps in a future career which took him to Hull, Manchester City, Sunderland and ultimately Leeds United) unhinged Pompey's previously rock-solid defence. However, the fact that his so-called smartness left Second Division defenders largely unmoved makes this an unlikely explanation. Others, such as Betty Rowse, who had patiently queued for her six-shilling ticket in one of the Highbury enclosures, blamed poor preparation. 'I was nearly in tears after they lost. The manager had them out walking before the match as the team all went to see the Boat Race in the morning. I think it might well have tired them all out.'

The most commonly held theory for the defeat, expounded to this day, was that there had been a bust-up in the dressing room shortly before kick-off when manager Jackson announced the team. 'I couldn't understand it when the teams ran out,' recounts supporter Mike Barnard. 'For one thing, Pompey were in red shirts and black shorts and as the players came out there were rumours around the ground there had been an argument in the changing room. Barlow had been picked ahead of Reid. For me Barlow was too old and Reid was extremely popular and had a great understanding with Clarke. As it was we got off on the wrong foot and we had no spark. No one had ever heard of this chap Revie.'

The expectation among supporters was that Pompey were destined for the 'double' and the players' shock failure needed some sort of rational explanation to explain an irrational result. Revie had given Leicester the lead after five minutes. Although Harris levelled before half-time, City regained the initiative two minutes into the second half. Eight minutes later it was all over as Pompey keeper Butler allowed Revie's header to slither from his grasp and over the line. Butler is also at pains to quash the pre-match bust-up theory. 'The result was just one of those things. There were so many stories about us arguing in the dressing room, but when the team was put up we just presumed that the manager's theory was that Barlow was better suited to the dry ground on the day. Duggie was more of a heavy-ground player, simple as that.' Butler's view was backed up by Len Phillips. 'The Barlow story was just an excuse. We never had a bust-up in the dressing room all the time I was there and Leicester just played above themselves. In any case, I can't imagine Duggie [Reid], the sort of bloke he was, wanting to argue.'

In fact, the result probably turned on an uncharacteristic miss by Harris, minutes before Revie's clinching goal. Six yards out and with the goal gaping, it seemed a formality to make the score 2-2. Instead, Harris's shot somehow screwed wide and Leicester were quick to take advantage. They were off to Wembley, where they would lose to Wolves.

That miss would haunt Harris for years. He was distraught for some days afterwards and asked to be left out of the team for the next match, a request that was predictably refused. The defeat also meant that supporter Peter Downton, who now lives in Rochester, Kent, had to eat a bit of humble pie. 'A friend of mine in London was an Arsenal supporter and he came down for the Jubilee match. To our delight he was devastated by the result: he spent most of the match with his mouth wide open. Unfortunately he managed to get a ticket to the semi-final and so had his revenge. My friend's smile returned and I was forced to drown my sorrows at Yates' Winebar in the Strand,' he recalled.

The question for Pompey was how this setback would affect their chances of a first League championship, now that the much-vaunted 'double' was off the agenda. 'Ranger' pondered what the psychological effects of the defeat would be and urged the team to give 100 percent effort to achieve their goal. The following Saturday, Liverpool were at Fratton Park. Full-back Jasper Yeuell was replaced by Bill Hindmarsh, who had been waiting patiently for his chance in the first team, having made just six League appearances since he signed professional almost ten years previously. His last appearance had been against Liverpool in November 1946, when he sustained a serious knee injury. By the 48th minute it seemed things were back to normal, as Clarke, Harris and Phillips established a three-goal cushion. However, the mid-table Merseysiders fought back strongly and goals from Albert Stubbins and wing-half Bob Paisley – who would become the most successful Liverpool manager ever – meant a tense finale. With the points in the bag, Pompey travelled to the north-east in good spirits for their vital clash with Newcastle. The Magpies were three points adrift of Pompey, having played a game more. Despite the fact that the match was played on a Wednesday afternoon, a crowd of more than 60,000 congregated at St James' Park, anticipating that by teatime the title race would have swung Newcastle's way.

How wrong could they be? Five headed goals – two from Harris and a hat-trick for Froggatt – had seemingly reduced the championship to a one-horse race. For absent Pompey supporters desperate for news of events in the north-east, they had few options. On Saturdays, the most reliable means of finding out how the team were doing away from home was to attend reserve matches at Fratton, where regular updates would be posted on the *Football Mail* scoreboard behind the Milton goal. Midweek matches – played in the afternoon in the absence of floodlights – were a different matter. Although wireless technology had expanded to feature a regular Saturday *Sports Report* on the BBC and Cup final commentaries, local radio would not come into being for another twenty years. The only source of information was the local newspaper, the *Evening News*. Its 'Final' edition, which would hit the streets around 4pm, would usually carry an account of the first half, and bits of the second if the game kicked-off earlier. Early second-half updates – and other half-time scores around the country – would be stencilled into the Stop Press column. However, those wanting the final score had to wait for the 'Special Final' edition in the early evening. This would include a full match-report, telephoned or wired by 'Ranger' to its offices in Stanhope Road. Also included would be the other results of the day and updated League tables.

Had Pompey won at Blackpool the following Saturday, those tables would have made exhilarating reading, but any hopes of extending Pompey's advantage were beached when the home side won 1-0. Although Rex Adams' goal looked offside, 'Ranger' accused the Pompey defence of not playing to the whistle. 'The goal that beat Pompey appeared to me to be one of the worst offside mistakes I have seen in years ... When the referee pointed to the centre spot there was an audible murmur of surprise right round the ground. Protests were useless ... but for me they only had themselves to blame because whatever their opinion may have been of Adams' position they should have played to the whistle and made a challenge. This they failed to do and paid the penalty,' he wrote in Monday's *Evening News*. To make matters worse, Newcastle rallied strongly after their shattering home defeat to win 4-2 at Derby. This meant that Pompey went into the crucial Easter routine of three games in four days still needing ten points from six games to be certain of the championship.

Since the inception of the Football League, the hectic Easter programme had been viewed as one of the defining moments of the season. The Good Friday/Saturday/Monday run of fixtures was widely regarded as being the ultimate test for teams seeking to carve their names on the honours board. The practice remained common until the 1980s. Back in 1902 a three-win holiday programme had been instrumental in Pompey clinching the Southern League title. Now, in 1949, the fixtures against Birmingham City, home and away, and at home to Wolves, looked set to settle Pompey's destiny.

Things didn't immediately go to plan as lowly Birmingham shocked almost 40,000 at Fratton by taking a first-half lead. But a brace of goals from Reid and another from Clarke kept the good ship Pompey on course for its destination. After the final whistle it emerged that Hindmarsh had played despite the fact that his wife was unwell in hospital. He had dashed to see her afterwards, but happily she was well enough for him to take his place for the following day's encounter with Wolves. Squad rotation had yet to enter football's lexicon and Jackson named an unchanged team. In front of a sun-baked, 'shirt-sleeved and cotton-frocked crowd,' according to 'Ranger', Pompey once and for all left no doubt about their claim to be the best in the land as the Cup finalists were put to the sword 5-0. Two goals in the first seven minutes set up the victory, which was embellished by a couple either side of half-time from Reid. The *coup de grace* – and Pompey's fiftieth home goal of the season – was claimed by Clarke with twenty minutes left. The match also exhibited a reminder of Reid's power shooting. Supporter Dave Randall regularly made the trip from Whitwell in the Isle of Wight – as did several hundred islanders – to watch Pompey. 'In that match against Wolves "Thunderboots" hit a shot from the edge of the area and the goalkeeper thrust up his arm and palmed it over the bar. Before the corner was taken, his reaction showed his hand was really throbbing. Reid's shot hurt. When he took a penalty, it was two paces back and ... bang.'

For the return at St Andrews on Easter Monday, an injury to Froggatt brought another recall for Parker, but that was the only change. If Pompey won and Newcastle went down at relegation-haunted Middlesbrough, the race for the championship would be all but over. The Magpies played their part, losing 2-3, despite leading 2-1 at half-time, but mid-table Birmingham had a shock in store for Pompey. Dickinson's badly cut head shortly before the interval meant he had to move out of harm's way, paradoxically up front, with Phillips dropping to left-half. The team, already trailing to John Stewart's 32nd-minute goal, never recovered and ended up losing 0-3.

Despite the setback, Pompey's fans refused to be downhearted, and as they made their way back to the south coast their enthusiasm drew comment from railway officials who wondered what would have happened had Pompey won. 'That is typical of the spirit of Portsmouth supporters this season and it has been responsible for much,' concluded 'Ranger' in his *Football Mail* column the following Saturday.

Ever since the win at Newcastle, Pompey had been designated champions-elect. However, silly dropped points had kept the champagne on ice. The team travelled up to Bolton determined to finally put the title beyond the grasp of the challenging pack. Dickinson's stitches had been removed from his head wound and he was passed fit to play. Clarke and Harris had each provided a goal for the other to put Pompey two up after 25 minutes, but the team were still relying on others dropping points to be absolutely certain of the crown. When Bolton's John Roberts poked home with eight minutes remaining, nerves were stretched to breaking point.

Dickinson's wound had re-opened, but there was no question of him going off and he finished the game with blood running down his face. Pompey survived and within minutes news filtered through that Newcastle and Manchester United had only drawn. Portsmouth were Champions of England. Chairman Vernon Stokes' optimistic rallying cry back in the summer had borne fruit with three matches to spare. It is a tribute to the recently nationalised British Railways' timetable – prior to Dr Beeching's swingeing cuts in the network – that on the way back from Bolton the team were able to change trains at Crewe in time to enjoy a celebratory meal in London that evening. The party then took a motor coach ride home to the city in the early hours of Sunday morning. They considered calling at Vernon Stokes' house – he had been at the Dell watching Southampton play that afternoon – but 'Ranger' wrote 'on second thoughts it appeared too unearthly an hour to call upon anybody, even to celebrate a championship victory.'

Of the directors, none was more proud than Syd Leverett, who had been involved with the club since its formation fifty years earlier. 'I saw them formed, I saw them in the mud, they came back, went on to win the Cup and now they have won the League championship. I have hoisted the oldest flag on the ocean, the Red Duster at my house. Now I am going to go to Fratton Park and get the club flag out, and it is going to stay out,' he said.

The presentation of the trophy had to wait seven days, when Mr E J Cearns of the Football League management committee was a guest in the directors box for the game with lowly Huddersfield. He was joined by Monty and the Lord Mayor of Portsmouth, Cllr Frank Miles. Before the match the championship flag was proudly unfurled to fly above the South Stand. Disappointingly for the player, Jimmy Dickinson was forced to miss his first match of the season. His head wound still hadn't healed, so his place went to Bill Thompson, a 27-year-old Scot who had signed from Carnoustie in March 1946, but who had yet to make a League appearance for the club.

It was ironic that Pompey's most famous son should be forced to miss the crowning glory of the season. Although he had only celebrated his 24th birthday six days previously, his style of play and supreme confidence on the football field had already marked him as one far more mature than his years. 'Gentleman Jim' was deceptively strong – his slight build and narrow shoulders seemingly gave him the appearance of a lightweight – and completely unflappable. His level-headedness and coolness under pressure meant that even nominally stronger players were unable to rattle him. In the late 1940s he sported a centre parting, which gradually shifted leftwards during his 21-year playing career at Fratton, a career which would never cause him to trouble the referee to ask for his name. Modest and shunning the limelight, Dickinson continued to live in his hometown of Alton, commuting to Fratton Park for work, right up until his heart attack in 1979, after which he was inevitably forced to take things somewhat easier.

It was a winning debut for Thompson. Huddersfield did their cause little good when George Hepplewhite handled in the box and Reid put his explosive right boot to good effect. However, it took until the 83rd minute for the points to be made safe, Clarke converting Reid's pass.

On the final whistle the crowd cascaded onto the pitch and thronged before the directors box. Skipper Flewin and his teammates emerged to receive the trophy from Mr Cearns, who told the crowd: 'I have always been impressed with your team's football. In addition to winning the championship they have created a record of which any team should be proud – that of being unbeaten at home.' The Football League only provided thirteen medals – two of which went to manager Jackson and trainer Stewart – so it was Butler, Rookes, Ferrier, the absent Dickinson, Flewin, Scoular, Harris, Barlow, Reid, Phillips and Froggatt who claimed the rest.

The number of medals issued was at the discretion of the Football League, 25 appearances being the usual requirement. The club, however, successfully sought permission from the League to have a special medal made for Clarke, who had missed games at the start of the season and only played in 24. Phil Rookes, who squeaked home with 25 to earn his medal holds the view that those presented to the manager and trainer really should have gone to players. Monty, too, praised the team and revealed that he had rescheduled a visit to France to ensure he was present at the game. 'Huddersfield won this Cup three times running. It is fitting that they should be here today to see Pompey win it for the first time after which they, too, will go on to win it three times,' he announced to loud cheers. In the early evening the team took to an open-topped bus – driven by long-time team chauffeur Bill Shepherd and preceded by the Fire Brigade band – to the Guildhall, past crowds six-deep lining the streets. 'Ranger' noted that scores of 'teen-agers' – perhaps the term is not a 1950s phenomenon after all – ran behind the bus all the way, one girl collapsing with exhaustion. At the Guildhall the players and officials enjoyed a civic reception, before adjourning to the Royal Beach Hotel, Southsea, for a celebration party. The only absentee was Bill Hindmarsh, who slipped away quietly with his sick wife.

Manager Jackson paid tribute to the Portsmouth supporters: 'I think they are simply marvellous. I thought they were enthusiastic in the north, but I must hand it to these people. No football crowd could have got so behind a team and kept them in front as the Pompey crowd have done this season,' he said, then added: 'It was my birthday on Friday and the lads in winning the championship have given me the best present I have ever had. I am the happiest man in football today.'

Although Pompey clearly had nothing to prove, their final two fixtures could scarcely have provided a sterner test: away at Arsenal on the Wednesday afternoon, then a visit to Manchester United on the final Saturday. Both matches would end in defeat – by the same margin of 2-3 – but on both occasions Pompey felt hard done by. For the game at Highbury, Pompey were deprived of winger Harris, who had been called up to represent the Football League against the Irish League. Parker replaced him. Injuries and fatigue also caught up with a team that had called upon just eighteen players all season. Thompson kept his place, this time because Harry Ferrier was resting a strained tendon. The Gunners rode their legendary good fortune that early spring evening, the game kicking off at 6.30pm. They also exploited the League rulebook to ensure that Pompey's speedy counter-attacking style would be somewhat slowed – by fair means or foul. Arsenal did not appear to take their dethronement graciously.

Since the Football League AGM of 1939, watering of pitches had been deemed permissible – except in November, December, January and February. But even so, supporters turning up to the game must have been somewhat surprised after a dry and mild April to see the Highbury playing surface a boggy morass. The pitch had had hoses on it all day. Pompey, naturally, had turned up with short studs in their boots 'while Arsenal had long ones in', recalled supporter Mike Barnard, who was living in London and went to the match. Despite their handicap, Pompey still led Arsenal a merry dance, but from Parker's header hitting the post early on, to Clarke having a late equaliser ruled out for an imperceptible handball, the gods certainly seemed to favour the deposed champions.

Fortune deserted Pompey again on the Saturday. The returning Harris had to hobble off shortly after Rowley had given Manchester United a 3-2 lead, leaving Pompey a man short. The lead had changed hands three times in an action-packed first half which ended all-square at 2-2. Pompey might have drawn 3-3, but Reid's reliability from the spot deserted him late on after a handball and United's victory allowed them to claim second spot for the third season in a row, five points behind Pompey's final total of 58. If nothing else, the keenness shown by both Arsenal and Manchester United to inflict defeat on the first team – and still the only team – south of the capital to claim a League title indicated the place Pompey now occupied in football's pecking order. Portsmouth were champions of England thanks largely to their collective spirit and belief in their own ability. They began the season as a team without stars. No longer. Dickinson, Harris, Froggatt, Scoular and the others were the best in the land and the rest of Division One would know what to expect next time around.

Pompey players relax playing bowls at Milton Park pre-season

Derby goalie Webster claims a cross from Froggatt, behind far post (March 1949)

Reg Flewin shakes hands with Derby skipper Howe, and ref Clark (March 1949)

The Pompey team depart to play Leicester in FA Cup semi-final (March 1949)

Harris scores Pompey's goal in the 1-3 semi-final defeat by Leicester (March 1949)

Liverpool's Done (No 10) receives attention, watched by ref Hartley (April 1949)

Liverpool's Bob Paisley guards the goal-line during this Pompey attack (April 1949)

Ike Clarke, on the floor with Wolves keeper Bert Williams, scores (April 1949).

6

The Team to Beat

May 1949 – November 1949

Season's end saw Pompey's championship achievements finally earn overdue international recognition when Jimmy Dickinson was called up for the England tour of Scandinavia, Holland and France from May 13-22. The schedule was acknowledged to be gruelling by the Football Association, who split the tour party into 'A' and 'B' squads. Dickinson started in the 'B' party, playing his part in a 4-0 win over Finland on 15 May on the 'hottest day of the year in Helsinki' according to the *FA Yearbook* for 1949-50. However, with the 'A' team having made a catastrophic start, losing 1-3 to Sweden in Stockholm, Pompey's left-half found himself promoted, making his full England debut against Norway in Oslo on 18 May. It proved to be little more than an exhibition game, as England won 4-1. Dickinson earned praise from all and sundry, hitting it off immediately with fellow defenders Neil Franklin and Billy Wright. It might have been a different story against France in Paris's Stade de Colombes on 22 May. Although Dickinson was not responsible, England let in a goal in 33 seconds, at the time believed to be the quickest goal the national side had ever conceded. England recovered their poise, winning 3-1.

Dickinson's globe-trotting was not yet done. Back in Sweden he rejoined a 21-strong party of Portsmouth team-mates and officials who were halfway through a five-match tour of Scandinavia. The reputation of English football had taken a battering in recent years and the Swedish press was confident the English champions would pose little threat to the combined Gothenburg Alliance side. The Swedish line-up was composed of players from three Swedish first division sides, including eight who had played in the recent win over England. Despite the fact that Pompey had already drawn 2-2 with the Danish national team and beaten Copenhagen 3-1, the Swedish writers brashly asserted that should the cream of English clubs compete in the Swedish league they would find themselves nearer the bottom than the top. English expatriates in Gothenburg ensured that these inflammatory comments reached the ears of Jackson, who used them to fire up his players. It did the trick. The Swedes were thrashed 4-2 – ending their ten-year unbeaten home run against foreign opposition – and the journalists were forced to eat their words. Thompson, standing in for the absent Dickinson, blotted out Gunnar Gren, the Swedish international, who admitted afterwards that Portsmouth were the best side he had ever played against. Pompey completed the tour unbeaten, recording 3-0 wins over a Jutland FA XI and another Copenhagen XI, then winding up with a 3-1 win in Belgium over Entente de Bruxelles.

When the team returned home, pre-season training was just seven weeks away. In late June the League fixtures for the new season were published. In those pre-computer days the fixture-list was compiled manually and its architects clearly possessed a sense of irony, sending the champions back to St James' Park, Newcastle, scene of their triumphant 5-0 eclipse of their title-pretending hosts just five months previously.

When the players reassembled for training, it was virtually a case of 'as you were', with no significant comings or goings. Once the late-summer ritual of sprints, lapping, bowls and strolls, with occasional training matches thrown in, was over, Pompey looked in pretty good shape. The obligatory public practice matches between the 'Reds' and the 'Blues' – which remained the closest that football in those days got to a pre-season friendly – provided an opportunity for the manager and training staff to fine-tune their preparations for the curtain raiser. These public trials were also major fund-raising opportunities for local charities. When the accounts were published in November 1949 (including £43 from the annual cricket match with the United Services) – £1,110 had been raised, with more than thirty charities benefiting. The club announced a record profit of £41,474 on a six-figure turnover for the first time ever. Chairman Vernon Stokes – who would be replaced by John Chinneck in September as part of a rotation system at the top, initiated in 1946 – was confident that another good season was in store. 'From the moment they first reported back for training there was a great keenness on the part of all the playing staff. The whole of the lads are determined to give of their best and we know what their best can be. Barring injuries we ought to have another good season,' he said. The books also revealed, oddly for a team that had just won the championship, a credit balance on transfers of £16,400. This was yet another tribute to the scouting network the club had built up over the years.

The Portsmouth team was still virtually self-selecting, with the right-back spot the only worry, as Rookes' ankle injury was slow to mend. Yeuell got the nod ahead of Hindmarsh for the opener at Newcastle, but manager Jackson's scouting network already had their eye on a possible replacement in Bradford's Jimmy Stephen – although the press was reporting that he might sign for Chelsea.

The rest of the team was familiar. Butler in goal, Ferrier the other full-back, Dickinson, Flewin and Scoular the half-backs, Froggatt and Harris on the wings, and Reid, Clarke and Phillips the forwards. Newcastle included forward George Robledo – a Chilean by birth – who had signed for the Geordies, along with his brother Edward from Barnsley the previous season. Today foreign players are an accepted part of the English game, and have been since 1978, when Tottenham secured work permits for Argentinian World Cup stars Osvaldo Ardiles and Ricky Villa. However, in the late 1940s foreigners of any description were still a novelty, as a player needed to have been resident in Britain for at least two years before he was eligible. Pompey had their own non national in Jamaican Delapenha, and the huge migration from eastern Europe as a result of the upheavals of World War II paved the way for what might have been an overseas invasion. The most notable of those who did break through was perhaps ex-German paratrooper Bert Trautmann, who risked his neck, literally, between Manchester City's goalposts in the 1956 FA Cup final. Trautmann had been playing non-league football for St Helens before signing for City in November 1949 and went on to make over 500 appearances for the club.

Any chance of Newcastle – foreign contingent notwithstanding – belittling Pompey's title quickly disappeared as first-half goals from Phillips and Clarke, then another after the break from Harris, put the game out of reach. Newcastle pulled one back, but Pompey had sounded a warning that they had no intention of surrendering their championship easily. 'Ranger' took delight in highlighting the fact that hundreds of Geordies were streaming home before the final whistle. The next two fixtures were at home to Manchester City and Blackpool. On paper – given Pompey's superlative home record the previous season – one could be forgiven for anticipating that the team would top the division after these first three fixtures. Instead, the week ended with serious questions being asked of their ability to defend their title.

On the Wednesday evening – there was sufficient natural light for matches in the summer and spring to kick off at around 6pm – Pompey hosted Manchester City, who had returned to the First Division in 1947. City had been relegated in 1938 in extraordinary circumstances. Not only had they been reigning League champions, but they went down having scored more goals (80) than they conceded (77). Indeed, they had been top scorers in the whole division! On their return in 1947 they had consolidated by finishing seventh. The champions' task seemed to have been made lighter by City's goalkeeping crisis. Frank Swift was injured, Bert Trautmann would not join them for another few weeks, so they were forced to draft in 19-year-old Ron Powell for his debut. The youngster ended up having an easy ride. Pompey hardly mustered a shot on target, save for Reid's converted penalty, and the visitors departed with a 1-1 draw.

On the Saturday a bumper crowd was anticipated for the visit of Blackpool and – more specifically – their mercurial winger Stanley Matthews. In the opposition's pen-pictures in the Pompey match programme his reputation preceded him. 'What can one say that supporters do not already know about the most magnetic player football has ever known?' was Matthews' entry. The Hanley-born son of a famous boxer had started his career with his hometown club Stoke in the 1930s and he had already earned himself pre-war England caps and the reputation as the wizard of the dribble. His transfer from Stoke to Blackpool in May 1947, at the age of 32, had not gone down well in the Potteries. He was still the biggest draw around at the time and if Stoke thought he was past his prime, they were made to rue their error. Matthews' career at Bloomfield Road would last until 1961, when he returned for a nostalgic – and productive – three seasons at the Victoria Ground, helping Stoke back to the First Division at the age of 49.

Against Pompey, however, Matthews had the reputation among local supporters for apparently feigning injury just before Blackpool's visit, so as to avoid tough-tackling, no-nonsense left-back Harry Ferrier. The evidence of the championship years would seem to dispel this myth, as Matthews played in both matches at Fratton Park, helping his side to claim three points out of four. Moreover, the stewards seeking to evenly distribute spectators on the terraces had an additional problem to contend with. 'Matthews had long hair and was quite scruffy in appearance for the time,' recalled supporter Mike Barnard, 'but if you ever went to see Blackpool, or Preston for that matter, the two corners of the ground down by the right wing were packed to see him, or Finney, in action.'

Matthews also showed his business acumen, as his day's work had started long before referee Thompson from Worksop set the game underway. Despite two pay-rises in the wake of football's unprecedented popularity in the immediate post-war years, players clearly were far from getting a fair share of the money flowing into the sport. To top up the maximum wage of £12, however, Matthews tried to exploit his name by promoting anything from Brylcreem hair-gel to cigarettes – the latter in spite of the fact he was a non-smoker! This particular August morning he was promoting his own brand of 'Co-operative' football boots – which he didn't wear – at the Fratton Road branch of that department store. Whatever boots he was wearing, they did the trick as Matthews gave Ferrier a torrid time. Blackpool stunned the 47,000 crowd by winning 3-2 to become the first team to leave Fratton Park with both points since Manchester United on Boxing Day 1947. For their part, Pompey felt aggrieved at having no fewer than three goals disallowed, which prompted 'Ranger' to query whether clubs should be allowed to appeal against bad decisions.

All of a sudden Pompey were enmeshed in a mini-crisis, losing 0-1 at Maine Road in the return with Manchester City despite creating, and wasting, numerous chances. After four matches the team were now in the bottom half of the table. With Delapenha recalled to the attack, a 5-1 win at Middlesbrough – which saw a thirteen-minute Harris hat-trick – seemed to have steadied the ship, only for Pompey to lose 0-1 at Aston Villa the next Monday. Everton arrived at Fratton having made a solid start, following a brush with relegation, and must have fancied themselves, despite conceding nine goals without reply in their two previous meetings with Pompey. Instead, they became the sacrificial lambs as Pompey roared to a 7-0 win – their biggest League win since beating QPR by the same score in 1924. Writing in the match programme beforehand, *Liverpool Echo* reporter Don Kendall reckoned: 'There is much individual distinction about this modern Everton, which has a defensive make-up comparable to the best in the land.' Rash words indeed! Reid – who returned after being dropped yet again – grabbed a hat-trick and prompted 'Ranger' to note that it was a pity he couldn't be rested more often. Reid's first goal, a fierce free-kick from the edge of the area, was featured in a frame-by-frame photo analysis in a football magazine, which speculated whether he might possess the hardest shot in the game.

Impatience at the team's turbulent early-season form prompted the usually loyal 'Ranger' to question whether now was the time for the club to splash out on a new forward. 'I do not believe any one of the Directors would go against his better judgement and disagree with me. The weak spots in the team are far too many and much too serious to be patched up. The truth is that better players must be found for certain positions both fore and aft. They are not in the reserve side and the only other source is via the chequebook,' he wrote in his column of 10 September.

Despite the Everton win, Pompey's season still refused to take off. Injury-hit Huddersfield were beaten 1-0 at Leeds Road and the Danish National XI defeated 6-2 in a midweek friendly at Fratton Park – although the visitors impressed with their technique. The invitation had been extended to the Danish football federation following the success of Pompey's pre-season tour of Scandinavia. Pompey that day were deprived of the services of Dickinson and Harris, both named in the England side to meet the Republic of Ireland at Goodison Park, Liverpool. It was to prove a watershed.

England's proud record of never having lost to an overseas team on home soil – though for some reason it is the Hungary defeat four years later that assumes that mantle in the public mind – was shattered by goals from Con Martin and Peter Farrell. Insular attitudes in the English game would mean the defeat was largely ignored – Martin was a centre-half with Aston Villa, after all, and Farrell a wing-half playing on his home ground – but it proved to be a devastating blow to Harris's international hopes. The 23-year-old right-winger was trying to muscle in on territory customarily dominated by Matthews and Finney, and despite his relative youth and superior goalscoring record, it would be five years before the selectors would call upon him again.

In the next home fixture, against Bolton, Montgomery was present, having his photograph taken with the team beforehand, but it proved to be 'one step back' as Pompey could do no better than draw 1-1. That same week some of the criticism directed at the team's reserve team backfired when they beat Arsenal – who fielded several first-teamers – 2-1 in a testimonial for ex-Brighton manager Charlie Webb at the Goldstone Ground. James Cairney, a 17-year-old centre-half recently signed from Strathclyde, was singled out for praise. The following Saturday, 1 October, Wolverhampton Wanderers were the visitors. Wolves were threatening to run away with the title, having won seven of their eight League matches and arrived in town fresh from slaughtering Huddersfield 7-1 at Molineux. For the first and only time, more than 50,000 spectators crammed into Fratton Park for a League match. On a sultry afternoon the St John Ambulance Brigade were kept busy dealing with cases of fainting. Come the end of the match, most of the crowd would have left crestfallen at the result. Reid's penalty was cancelled out in the second half by Jesse Pye, to leave Pompey in seventh place, three points behind Wolves. Evidence that the board was becoming twitchy was highlighted by the fact that director Syd Leverett and trainer Jimmy Stewart missed the game to go on a scouting mission in the West Country.

The following week Pompey took their first team to Scotland for a short break. While they were there they beat Scottish 'A' division side Clyde 3-0 in a friendly in front of 20,000, but were delayed on their return journey by train problems at Crewe and arrived at Birmingham late, although in good time for the 3pm kick-off at St Andrews.

Harris showed he had lost none of his sparkle, despite his international setback, laying on three first-half goals, two for Clarke and one for Reid. The 3-0 win would have delighted the Portsmouth contingent in the 38,000 crowd who had taken advantage of a British Railways special excursion costing 21s 3d (£1.06), which departed from Fratton at 8.51am and returned at 11.20pm. That afternoon also saw Pompey's championship achievement marked in unusual style: Birmingham City director John Woolman – a noted chrysanthemum grower – announced he would be exhibiting a new variety named 'Portsmouth' at a Chrysanthemum Show to be staged in the Wesley Central Hall Fratton, at the end of the month.

One possible reason for Pompey's slow start was the difficulty in fielding a settled side. Twelve months previously, just twelve players were fielded in their first sixteen League matches. In fact the same eleven were fielded fourteen times. For the Derby match at Fratton on 15 October, Reg Pickett – the wing-half signed from Weymouth in January – became the fourteenth player used so far. He replaced Jimmy Dickinson, whose international reputation was unscathed by England's defeat by the Republic of Ireland, and who now took his place in the England side that would beat Wales 4-1 at Cardiff in the Home International Championship cum World Cup qualifier. Back then, football clubs had to put a brave face on international call-ups, much like cricket counties must to this day. There was no chance of Pompey seeking a postponement of the Derby fixture just because their best player happened to be in demand by his country.

It would turn out a day of double celebration, as even without their talisman Pompey still proved too good for the Rams, winning 3-1. The match programme that afternoon appealed for supporters to show consideration in assisting the stewards and police to pack the crowds at home games more effectively. Following discussions between the club and the police, an appeal was made for supporters to keep gangways clear: 'Those spectators who make a practice of sitting on the terracing are creating a danger ... Immediately a game commences they stand up and cause blank spots and should the crowd start swaying there can be trouble.'

In that evening's *Football Mail*, Pompey championship neckties were advertised for sale priced 7s 4d (37p) at Landports Drapery Bazaar – now Allders – in Commercial Road, along with ladies headscarves in Pompey's colours. In those days the merchandising of football had yet to take root. The typical supporter's apparel in the late 1940s (through to the 1960s and even 70s) consisted of a knitted scarf or 'muffler' in coloured segments and a rosette bought from sellers dotted around the ground offering colours from both sides pinned on their boards. Another line in early merchandise was lapel-badges featuring a miniature likeness of a player set in a round frame. These have become collectors' items in recent years. John Phillips recalls a seller at the top of Frogmore Road with badges and rosettes pinned to a board, but the club itself had no official shop until the late 1960s! The players, too, found a way of supplementing their wages. Eleven of them commissioned Portsmouth photographers Wright and Logan to take studio portraits, prints of which were then sold privately to supporters. Full-back Phil Rookes, who at that time was still recuperating from an ankle injury, was the brains behind this idea. 'We charged a shilling for a team picture and 6d (2½p) for the individuals. The club gave us the necessary permission and we included Bob Jackson and Jimmy Stewart in on the rewards. I had a heck of a job to get the lads to sign the team photos! I gave them a hundred at a time, piles of them, but they had a nice nest egg at the end of the season. I sent a letter, plus a set of photos to the sports editors of all the provincial newspapers in England and they printed the information, plus a glowing report on the quality of the pictures – youngsters from all over sent in,' he added proudly.

The relative lack of memorabilia and souvenirs, it must be said, also added to the sense of occasion on a match-day. 'When I stood on the North Terrace opposite the tunnel,' explained Cyril Lucas, 'I couldn't wait until the players came up the tunnel. I was just so full of pride when I saw those royal blue shirts and that star and crescent badge. That shirt was only worn by the eleven players – no one else wore it, unlike the replica shirts you see these days – and you wouldn't see it again until the next match. It was Pompey's pride and glory and a huge cheer went up when the players ran out.'

Before their next League appointment, away at newly promoted West Bromwich Albion, Pompey had a date with the FA Charity Shield. This match traditionally pits the champions against the FA Cup winners, with the gate proceeds going to 'good causes' – whatever that might mean. In 1949 champions Pompey were to renew their acquaintance with League leaders Wolves, who had beaten Leicester 3-1 in the Cup final in April. Unlike today, where the fixture is the showpiece start to the football season – and since 1974 staged at Wembley – in 1949 the fixture was scheduled for the afternoon of Wednesday, 19 October at Highbury. Inevitably the crowd would be small, and although Pompey outsold their Midlands rivals by three to one, there were still only around 25,000 spectators scattered around the 65,000-capacity stadium by kick-off. Despite taking a first-half lead through Reid, Pompey couldn't hold on. Ferrier was adjudged to have handled – harshly it seemed – and Hancocks converted the penalty. The game ended 1-1 and although the silverware went back on the train to Portsmouth that night, six months later it passed to the Molineux boardroom. According to custom, following a draw the trophy was shared.

Pompey paid a heavy price for their participation, as Harris and Clarke picked up knocks that would keep them out of Saturday's game. And when Reid and Phillips went down with flu, it was very much a scratch side that reported for duty at the Hawthorns. Pickett moved to inside-forward, Parker and Barlow made their first appearances of the season at left-wing and inside-left respectively, and a debut was handed to James Dawson, a 21-year-old forward who had signed from Leicester during the summer. It was to prove his one and only Pompey appearance.

The crowd at West Brom were disappointed to learn that their former favourite, Ike Clarke, was unfit and unable to play for Pompey. They soon cheered up as their favourites, kicking with a stiff breeze in the first half, raced into a 2-0 lead, which was extended to 3-0 in their first meeting with Pompey in ten years. With leaders Wolves losing at Manchester United, a perfect opportunity to close the gap had been squandered. It also meant Pompey had now used eighteen players, the same total as used in the whole of the previous season, and it was not yet November. The following week another debutant – reserve centre-half Bill Spence – was drafted in to replace the injured Thompson, but with most of the other absentees returning Pompey held Manchester United to a 0-0 draw. Pompey were indebted to Pickett, who cleared a United effort off the line in the second half.

Come November, Portsmouth's directors finally bought a player to shore up the defence, offering Second Division strugglers Bradford Park Avenue around £10,000 for their 27-year-old Scottish international right-back Jimmy Stephen. With Rookes on the long-term injury list, Hindmarsh and Yeuell had been covering for him, but not to the satisfaction of the management. At the time the signing of Stephen was a record cash deal for a full-back. Although Alf Ramsey's recent transfer from Southampton to Tottenham had been valued higher, at £18,000, it included a player exchange. As it turned out, several months would pass before Pompey could call on their new acquisition on a regular basis as Stephen was completing his National Service in the Royal Air Force. He had been spotted by Pompey scouts playing in a representative match between the RAF and the Football League – whose side, incidentally, included Chesterfield's future Pompey winger, Gordon Dale.

Stephen recalled: 'I knew there were representatives from Portsmouth at the match to watch me and after the match manager Bob Jackson and one of the directors, I think it was Harry Wain, came up to me and said they would like to sign me. I must have hesitated, because they immediately said that I would be joining a good club, that I'd be on top money when I left the RAF and that they would buy me a house too. They asked me where I was stationed and they arranged to meet me that Friday outside the main gate of the camp at 5pm. Unfortunately, at St Athan, in

South Wales where I was based, there were two sites and I reported to the wrong gate, but soon a message telling AC Stephen to report to the other gate came over the Tannoy and that was it. I signed. I think Bradford upped the fee a little bit, because Pompey were such a big club at the time.'

Having paid such a handsome fee for an international player – his two appearances for Scotland had seen him captain his side in the 1-3 defeat by Wales at Wrexham in October 1947 – one might have expected that Jackson would call on him at once. However, things didn't quite work that way in the late 1940s. Stephen wasn't due to be demobbed until February 1950 and until then (can you imagine Sir Alex Ferguson or Arsene Wenger putting up with such an imposition?) the RAF had first call on his time. Stephen was able to obtain a weekend pass to make his debut for the reserves at Swindon on 12 November and another a fortnight later for his first-team debut, but until the spring his appearances at Fratton would be restricted.

And that had an adverse effect on Stephen's income too. 'I could only earn £6 a game, whether it was first team or reserves, and I couldn't sign a full contract until I left the services. However, I was ambitious and wanted First Division football. I had asked to be transfer listed at Bradford many times and it was finally granted during my National Service. I was approached by several clubs, including Hull and Southampton, but I wasn't interested as they were still Second Division.'

Pompey's form continued to blow hot and cold, but left-winger Froggatt was in fine fettle in front of the watching England selectors at Chelsea on 7 November. He scored twice in a 4-1 win and set up one of the other goals. Froggatt's reward came soon afterwards as he made his England debut in the 9-2 thrashing of Northern Ireland at Maine Road on 16 November, scoring one of the goals.

The flaxen-haired Froggatt, who had been born in Sheffield, but whose family had moved south to set up a butcher's shop in Portsmouth, had a quite different style of wing-play to his partner Harris, but no less effective. Known as 'Jolly Jack', reflecting his good-natured demeanour, Froggatt was a well-built, barrel-chested individual, who used his strength to good effect, frequently dominating an opponent. His physique also made him a useful utility player, enabling him to switch to centre-forward should the need arise. In the latter stages of his Pompey career he would become an international centre-half, making the position his own, having filled in there after Reg Flewin was injured in January 1951. Despite eventually moving to Leicester, in March 1954 at the age of 32, he returned to Portsmouth after he retired from the game to run a number of public houses in the city, including the Manor House and the Milton Arms. He retired to West Sussex where he lived until his death in 1993.

The Chelsea match had been played in torrential rain, which reduced the crowd to 31,000, several thousand of whom came from the south coast. It was a straightforward rail journey from Portsmouth to Waterloo and from there by Underground to Fulham Broadway. It was also, as Betty Rowse recalled, a chance to take tea and Dundee cake in the Waterloo refreshment bar, before catching the 6.20pm return train to Portsmouth. When they got home to read the *Football Mail*, which was sold by young boys at stations and on the streets throughout the evening, they would have seen a League table which had Pompey in fifth place, five points adrift of pace-setters Wolves.

If they thought such a fine result would act as a springboard, they were wrong. The following Saturday lowly Stoke, who had shocked Wolves 2-1 a week before, ground out a 0-0 draw at Fratton Park, with only the performance of Dickinson – following the announcement that he had been omitted from the England squad to face Northern Ireland – earning anything like praise. Indeed, had a shot from Stoke's John Malkin been a shade more accurate (it hit the woodwork), alarm bells would have rung. However, the game was contested with a fierce gale blowing from end to end, which prompted a national newspaper to claim it would have been fairer to the paying supporters if the match had been postponed on account of the wind.

Pompey were, at the time, trying to sign Sheffield Wednesday forward Eddie Quigley, who had found himself on the sidelines at Hillsborough, but the deal looked likely to founder on the Second Division club's insistence on a player-exchange rather than a straight cash deal. Some weeks earlier Pompey's interest in Leicester's transfer-listed Don Revie, who had scuppered their 'double' aspirations the previous spring, had come to nothing because of similar demands.

Pompey succumbed to their habitual defeat at Turf Moor, 1-2, in which future Burnley manager Harry Potts scored the deciding goal, and went into their match with Sunderland the following Saturday without Hindmarsh, Clarke and Scoular, all of whom were injured. Manager Jackson was forced into another reshuffle, fielding three debutants – Stephen (on a 48-hour leave pass), Perth-born Jimmy Elder at wing-half, and Swedish international forward Dan Ekner, who had signed on amateur forms in October while working for his company in England. Ekner's amateur status meant he could evade the two-year 'residency' regulation required by the Football Association for non-British citizens who hoped to play in England. For Elder it was to be his only-ever appearance for Pompey, having signed for the club in September 1945 from Scottish junior football.

Opposing Pompey that day was Sunderland's centre-forward and self-styled 'Clown Prince' of the English game, Len Shackleton. His blank chapter in his autobiography, *The Clown Prince of Soccer* published in 1955, entitled 'What the average Director knows about football' remains a landmark comment on the feudal nature of soccer management at that time. Shackleton happened to be a friend of Stephen, whom he met at Bradford Park Avenue where they both started their careers before the war. Indeed, Stephen made his full debut as a 17-year-old at the start of that fateful 1939-40 season. The bond had strengthened in the post-war period, when the two men were drafted down the mines as 'Bevin Boys', as the newly elected Labour Government sought to address a national coal shortage.

The friendship helped Stephen to make a solid start to his Pompey career: 'Len realised that I was making my First Division debut for Pompey and early on there was a 50:50 challenge at the Fratton End, halfway between the penalty area and the touchline. As we shaped up I saw it was Len out of the corner of my eye and he shouted "Yours Jimmy!" It was a spontaneous gesture of friendship and I really appreciated that he was, for that moment, prepared to put me before his club.' Unfortunately the friendship only went so far, as it was Shackleton's 47th-minute goal which pulled his team back into a match in which they had trailed 0-2 at half-time. A minute later Ivor Broadis – an England international who would go on to establish himself as one of the north-east's top football journalists – equalised. Pompey had squandered another precious point.

The following Saturday the team travelled to Anfield to meet the undefeated current leaders Liverpool – who had opened up a three-point gap at the top of the table and who were eight points ahead of seventh-placed Pompey. It was a game the team simply could not afford to lose if their hopes of becoming the first club to retain the title since Arsenal in 1934-35 were to remain intact.

Part of the crowd to watch the civic reception for Pompey (April 1949)

Pompey chairman R Vernon Stokes (far left) toasts the champions (April 1949)

Reg Flewin holds the championship trophy, with Monty's approval (April 1949)

Hundreds of Pompey fans at Fratton Park offer their congratulations (April 1949)

The championship team leaves Fratton Park on an open-top bus (April 1949)

Montgomery arrives at the Guildhall for the championship reception (April 1949)

Wearing new blazers and crest, Pompey players leave for Scandinavia (May 1949)

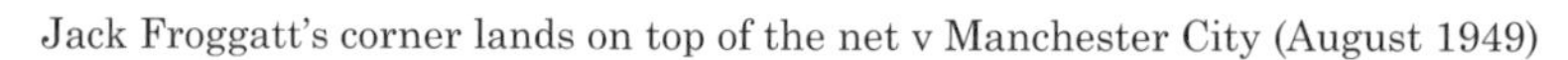
Jack Froggatt's corner lands on top of the net v Manchester City (August 1949)

7

Days of Doubt

November 1949 – February 1950

Manager Bob Jackson prepared his team for the crunch match at Liverpool in the face of crippling injury worries. Spence continued to deputise for Flewin, although the skipper was approaching full fitness after having had his appendix removed back in September. Ekner, too, kept his place, despite Phillips' return after a bout of tonsillitis, as Reid was ruled out by an injury picked up the week before. Damp weather in the south that week probably restricted training to a monotonous routine of shuttle runs under the shelter of the North Stand. Despite being reigning English champions, at that time Pompey didn't have their own training ground and all training took place at Fratton. Inclement weather would immediately render the pitch unusable and the only 'ball work' possible would be 'head tennis' performed after training behind the Fratton End in a small open space near to the offices. This competitively undertaken event usually pitted the English – Dickinson, Froggatt, Harris and the like – against the Scots, who could count on Reid, Ferrier and Scoular among others.

An average training week saw players report to Fratton on a Monday to receive their wages and clean their boots from the previous Saturday's match. The Tuesday, Wednesday and Thursday would have morning sessions dedicated to the usual diet of lapping the pitch, usually six times, and sprints. Friday would comprise a lighter session of perhaps a couple of laps and some sprints. Strange as it may seem, the conventional training wisdom of the time was to purposefully avoid ball-work. The theory was that having been deprived of the ball during the week, the players would be hungry for it on a Saturday.

'The emphasis was on maintaining fitness, as you should have done the stamina work with road running in pre-season training and when we did get the ball we would only play practice matches. We didn't work on our technique at all,' recalled Jimmy Stephen. 'In those days, though, the positions were very stereotyped and it was easy to slot into a team. When I made my debut for Pompey, I had been put up in the Royal Beach Hotel on Southsea seafront before the game and I walked to the ground, arriving the required three-quarters of an hour before the kick-off. It was the first-team trainer, Jimmy Easson, who introduced me to the players – I'd never trained with them or even met most of them. The players on the pitch, if you like, decided any "tactics". We would sort things out and adapt to circumstances on the field.'

When the team arrived at Anfield on 3 December to face Liverpool, torrential rain had reduced the pitch to a swamp. 'Ranger' in the *Football Mail* reported that the respective goalkeepers stood in their own 'private ponds'. Though the centre-circle was submerged, forcing the toss-up to take place on the touchline, this was not enough to persuade referee Iliffe from Leicester that the pitch was unplayable. However, the match – like the aquatic pitch – ebbed and flowed furiously, and when Clarke drove home to level Cyril Done's second goal to earn a 2-2 draw, Pompey's collective self-belief in their role as serious title challengers had been restored. 'Ranger' commented on some idiosyncratic positional play by the Swede Ekner: 'I thought his marking for a throw-in a little strange according to the English style. This, of course, is something that can be quickly remedied and no doubt will be.' Quite.

However, it was necessary that Pompey keep up the pressure by beating Arsenal at Fratton the following Saturday. The Gunners had assumed their habitual position in the top four, and although Flewin was recalled, the portents didn't look good. First Scoular was ruled out with a sore knee – two weeks rest were the doctor's orders – and then Peter Goring gave Arsenal a fourth-minute lead. Fortune proceeded to smile on Pompey as the London side scorned a host of chances to put the game out of reach, only to succumb to Clarke's glancing header with twelve minutes to go. Froggatt converted a simple chance five minutes later to secure Pompey's first win at Fratton in six long weeks and, more importantly, it kept the team in touch with the leaders. Compared with the previous season, however, the team were already four points down at the equivalent stage. Nevertheless, they say the mark of a good team is its ability to win when playing poorly and this performance could be cited as evidence for that.

The club tried again to reinforce the squad, making another attempt to lure Sheffield Wednesday's Eddie Quigley, who had now fallen out with the Yorkshire club over their reluctance to find him an additional job to supplement his income. 'We are a football club, not an employment agency,' was their tart riposte. However, it soon became apparent that despite averaging crowds in excess of 35,000, the Pompey directors were ill-inclined to break the bank to shore up what was evidently a problem position in the forward line. Wednesday were not prepared to accept Pompey's valuation of Quigley and he eventually moved to Preston for £26,500.

The team's ability to grind out results was reinforced by a 1-0 victory over Newcastle at Fratton. The win was down to Clarke's knack of being in the right place at the right time. Only three minutes had elapsed when defender Batty's clearance off the line deflected into the net off the centre-forward. However, skipper Reg Flewin deserves a mention in dispatches. He played the last five minutes in a daze after being knocked out in blocking George Robledo's late rocket. The result produced a bottle-neck at the top of the table, as leaders Liverpool went down at Sunderland, only their second defeat of the season. Just four points now separated Liverpool from seventh-placed Pompey. *Daily Express* pundit Alex James, the former Arsenal forward, considered Pompey were a good bet still for the title. 'Maybe they haven't got the bite of last season, but they play good methodical football, the kind of stuff that is going to put them in the running again,' was his verdict on the Newcastle game. Clarke, too, drew praise from 'Ranger' in Monday's *Evening News*: 'In spite of being in his middle 30s he turned out some football which would have made some of the young ones envious. He has certainly repaid his transfer fee, whatever it was, and is as dangerous at centre-forward as inside-forward.'

The win over Newcastle set Pompey up for the tough Christmas and New Year schedule, so beloved by the British game, starting at Bloomfield Road, Blackpool on Christmas Eve, which in 1949 fell on a Saturday. It would be another 25 years before the Football Association would sanction Sunday football, so in 1949 professional footballers enjoyed the rare luxury of Christmas Day at home, apart from those who played for Hull City. They had to travel down to London to prepare for their Boxing Day fixture at Brentford. However, players up and down the country could hardly afford to over-indulge. On 26 December Pompey would play the first of their 'double-headers' with Charlton at the Valley, with the return 24 hours later.

There was no great secret about how players handled such a punishing schedule. 'You just had to look after yourself,' explained Ernie Butler. 'You simply couldn't have a late night or a drink and besides there were plenty of rules and regulations we had to abide by, such as being in by 10.30pm every night and not being able to drive a car. If you were a player living in digs, Jimmy Stewart, the head trainer would check up on you. I can remember having to keep a look out if my wife Evelyn and I had been to the pictures for the evening. The bus didn't get back until 10.50pm and we had to walk to our house in Bonchurch Road, which is just round the corner from Fratton Park.' Len Phillips also remembers the strict regime. 'The trainers used to come round to players' houses or digs to check up about 10pm. I used to go to the Savoy in Southsea to see the big bands and I sometimes went there on a Friday night. Bob Jackson walked in one evening and said: "What are you doing here?" I told him I didn't drink and I was just listening to the music to take my mind off the game the next day. He was all right about it, as I told him I knew he had people here. The manager of the Savoy used to sit in his office and watch what was going on and report back.'

No seasonal gifts were handed out to Pompey by the seaside. Blackpool – including Matthews – consolidated their title challenge with a 2-1 victory and completed a prized double over the reigning champions. Indeed, Blackpool were fast becoming a bogey team for Pompey, as they had now failed to beat the Seasiders in the last nine attempts. However, Pompey could console themselves on the long train journey home – via connections at Manchester and London – with the experiences of an unnamed Blackpool player. He recounted the tale afterwards of how he had consulted one of the ladies who gaze into crystal balls on the promenade. Having crossed her palm with silver, no doubt, he would have been disappointed to hear he wasn't going to get a medal this season, and all she could see coming up before her eyes was the name 'Portsmouth'. Perhaps there is something in this gypsy soothsaying lark after all.

Inspired maybe, Pompey bounced back at the Valley, where Phillips gave them the lead just before the interval. Froggatt then doubled it on the hour. Charlton's fight-back was too little, too late, although Charlie Vaughan's late goal did set up a tense finish. The crowd of almost 38,000 at the Valley also contributed to a new League record of 1,226,098 spectators for a full day's programme in the four divisions, although even that record had just 24 hours to last before it was supplanted by a new figure of 1,253,572. Golden times indeed for football. Making his debut in the Charlton side on Boxing Day afternoon was 21-year-old centre-half Malcolm Allison, who was given a testing time by Clarke. 'Big Mal' would go on to make more than 250 appearances for West Ham and carve out a managerial name at Manchester City and Crystal Palace, but supporter Mike Barnard also remembers playing with him during their Army National Service. Both men were serving in the Royal Hampshire Regiment. Barnard used to help organise coaches to take supporters to games at Fratton Park during the first championship season from their camp in Wiltshire.

The next day it was back to the reserves for Malcolm Allison, who was dropped by Charlton for the return. Hundreds of Charlton fans missed out on the big match as well. A strike of electric train drivers meant that no services operated between Waterloo and

Portsmouth. Those frustrated Charlton fans missed a brave display by their team, but once again Pompey dug deep and Harris's header conjured up the winning goal immediately after half-time. As was their wont, four days later Pompey scorned the opportunity to build on their resilience when mid-table Middlesbrough stole a point at Fratton. The home side's offside trap failed to spring, leaving Peter McKennan to run on and plant an equaliser past Butler. Up in the stands that day was D Lochhead, the manager of Third Division (South) Norwich City, who had pulled out the 'plum' FA Cup Third Round draw – away to champions Pompey.

In 'Ranger's' interim review of the season he pointed the finger squarely at the team's poor home form, which had seen them drop eight points in twelve matches at Fratton, compared with three from thirteen the previous season. A comparable record this time around would have seen Pompey back on top of the table. Concern was also expressed – not for the first time – about the lack of punch up front. Rectifying this weakness was seen as the key to a second championship. 'With the team as it is today I don't think it [the title] is possible, but if they can get a thrustful player for the attack I can see them having a very good shot at it. But that new player for the attack is essential before Pompey can hope to be capable of making a real challenge for the championship.' Ekner was judged 'too dainty' for the heavy grounds and Delapenha, despite having some 'nice touches' lacked the 'devil' required to make the attack the force it should be. Even Reid's return from injury 'hadn't provided the solution,' 'Ranger' concluded.

Norwich had not visited Fratton Park for 26 years, since Billy Haines' hat-trick helped Pompey to a 4-0 win on their march to the Third Division (South) championship. Since then the two clubs' respective fortunes had diverged, so that Portsmouth went into the game short-priced favourites.

The absence of any information in the programme about possible replay arrangements perhaps hinted at over-confidence, and Norwich, who were handily placed for a tilt at promotion in fourth place, were intent on making the most of their day, which dawned sunny and 'spring-like'. Almost 10,000 supporters made the journey from East Anglia. One of them, 17-year-old Tom Davies – the son of a Norfolk vicar – cycled the 200 miles or so overnight. The City directors were so impressed by his devotion they gave him a ride home on the team bus. The Norwich team had conformed to Cup tradition, retreating to Bournemouth for some bracing sea air to prepare for the big match and on the day they didn't disappoint. In their specially-made canary-yellow silk shirts, Norwich were far from overawed and seemed to be justly aggrieved when Delapenha appeared to handle as his attempted header from Ferrier's cross flew into the net. The Canaries were back on song on the hour, however, Noel Kinsey nipping in ahead of Butler to poke home a short back-pass.

That goal earned Norwich a money-spinning replay. Pompey's shoddy performance at Fratton, however, provoked a torrent of criticism in the letters column of the *Football Mail*. One irate fan, hiding under the *nom-de-plume* 'Heart Broken' of Copnor, vented his spleen: 'I think this was a disgusting show for a first division team. Almost 20 years at the Park and I have never seen anything like it ... If Pompey want to make a show in the Cup or league they have to go out and buy a couple of forwards in my opinion. I reckon Pompey are the meanest club of all divisions for paying out, and may I finish up, if Pompey do not win on Thursday [the replay], my old woman will be having more of my company on Saturday afternoons in the future.'

Others were equally critical, also threatening never to set foot inside Fratton again. 'Ranger' conveyed these letters to the board and received the familiar reply: 'be patient'. An unnamed director added: 'There are over 200 players on the market and we have had all of those worth considering watched but there is not one of them better than we have got on our books. You can tell your readers that if any one of them can tell us where there is a player better than we have who is for transfer, without parting with one of our own best players, we will go and get him whatever the price.' Manager Jackson noted that even the England selectors could not find the 'thrustful' inside-forwards the national team needed. 'All they have to do is name them and they are theirs ... but they cannot find the men they want.'

The replay at Carrow Road was scheduled for Thursday afternoon to take advantage of early closing day in the Norfolk city. In those times it was customary for shop-staff to work a five and a half day week. As Saturday was a busy shopping day, shops would close at lunchtime one day in midweek, usually Wednesdays or Thursdays.

The Pompey squad took advantage of an overnight stay in London to attend a show, at which director Harry Wain, a fruit and vegetable merchant, caused much amusement by being dared to go on stage with the female members of the cast. Several hundred Pompey fans also took advantage of a special train put on for the match. Unfortunately, it broke down en route to Norfolk and by the time it arrived the gates had closed on a new ground record of more than 42,000. Attempts to set up a live radio broadcast to the thousands thronging outside failed to materialise and Portsmouth FC ended up receiving angry letters from supporters, especially as the train home lacked a refreshment car! At least they could console themselves with the knowledge that a second-half brace from Duggie Reid had carried Pompey through to the fourth round, where they would entertain Second Division Grimsby. The outcome might, however, have been different had referee Bond allowed a Norwich goal with five minutes remaining, when Kinsey saw his shot hacked off the line by Ferrier. Despite a deputation of City players urging him to consult his linesman, the official remained unmoved and a corner was awarded instead.

Pompey had just one day to prepare for their trip to Goodison Park to face Everton on 14 January. A knock picked up by Froggatt meant that Cliff Parker, by now 36 years old, was drafted in on the left wing for only his second appearance of the season. Having lost their previous three matches to Portsmouth, conceding sixteen goals without reply, the Toffees must have been more shocked than most when John Grant scored after Pompey had failed to clear a corner shortly before half-time. When Phillips headed in a free-kick after the hour – despite Reid having left the field for fifteen minutes to be treated for an injury – it provoked a rare instance of crowd trouble. Police were summoned to deal with an Everton supporter who had been so incensed at referee Roger's decision to award the free-kick from which Phillips scored, that he had thrown a missile at him. The decisive goal went Pompey's way when Harris converted Clarke's cross, the win keeping the team in touch with new leaders Manchester United.

The club had been due to host a prestige friendly against Argentine side Racing Club on Monday, 18 January. The South American team was touring Spain and Portugal, and the Football Association invited the party to come to England to play two fixtures against the champions and Cup winners, Wolves. Sadly, both games were cancelled when the respective FAs failed to reach agreement over expenses payable to the Argentinians.

Pompey were at last performing with reasonable consistency, with just one defeat in twelve League and Cup matches. That tally soon stretched to thirteen as Monty, alongside the Admiral of the Fleet, saw Huddersfield soundly beaten 4-0 at Fratton Park on 21 January. Seven days later Grimsby's hopes of a Cup upset were left in tatters as the home side romped to a 5-0 win. February 1950 was shaping up as a crucial month for Pompey's fortunes. After seven consecutive home ties, dating back to January 1947 when Brighton had been pulled out of the bag, Pompey's FA Cup 'luck' now deserted them. And how. The fifth round draw required a trip to table-topping Manchester United. The tie was sandwiched between League visits to lowly Bolton and a Wolves side which had wobbled since the autumn and were now slipping out of contention. The month would close with a visit from struggling Birmingham, at which point it would be apparent if Pompey had any realistic hopes of keeping their crown.

Things didn't start well at Burnden Park. Reid missed a penalty after just eight minutes, after the goalkeeper had brought him down. Then, late on, Phillips saw his shot come back off the bar. In between those misses Bolton's Nat Lofthouse headed home after a goalmouth scramble. That defeat severely dented Pompey's championship aspirations and meant that the Cup trip to Old Trafford offered the more likely route to glory. Interest in the tie was extraordinary. Several thousand Pompey fans planned to make the trip north. Tickets went on sale the Sunday after the Bolton game, with police warning supporters in the *Football Mail* not to start queuing before 8am.

That cup-tie at Old Trafford was an epic, pitting together the top two teams in the country. Yet again an injury forced Pompey to re-jig their attack, Reid's damaged leg forcing him to stay at home. Froggatt moved to centre-forward and the mercurial Parker came in at left-wing. Phillips hit a post for Pompey early on, only for United to score twice through Charlie Mitten's shot and a header from Stan Pearson. Within three minutes of the turnaround the game was transformed as Clarke poached a goal from close range, then sixty seconds later the veteran Parker headed home Harris's cross for 2-2. The game ended with two successful penalties, one apiece. Mitten netted for United following Ferrier's handball, but Ferrier made amends from the spot after Allenby Chilton also handled. After the match hundreds of Pompey fans surrounded the team bus to congratulate the players on a job well done before dashing to catch their own connection to London.

Monday's Cup draw offered the replay winners a quarter-final trip to either mid-table Chelsea or Third Division (North) Chesterfield. That Wednesday replay at Fratton saw the gates locked with almost 50,000 inside. Arrangements were made for Police Inspector Saunders to relay a commentary to the thousands locked out. Parker continued to deputise in the absence of Reid, and ultimately Pompey's lack of attacking strength in depth proved costly. United raced into two-goal lead through Mitten and Johnny Downie, a £16,500 reserve signing from Bradford. Although Harris pulled one back before half-time, Delaney sealed United's place in the last eight immediately after the restart. Afterwards manager Jackson conceded that the better team had won: 'The players are naturally disappointed but never mind, we must have a good crack at the League. We've still got a good chance of winning the championship again.'

To do so, however, would require the team to sustain the consistency shown of late, starting the following Saturday at Wolves, whose early season form had deserted them. It seemed a winnable match, with Wanderers forced to reshuffle their front line and giving fourteen-stone full-back Angus McLean his first game as centre-forward. Perhaps Pompey underestimated their opponents for they fell behind after seven minutes when McLean glanced home Mullen's corner. Despite Pompey having chances to salvage something, Wolves keeper Bert Williams was equal to them and another precious couple of points had slipped away.

Pompey were about to notch up another of those innovative firsts for which they were to become renowned over the years. In response to criticisms that spectators and players alike were sometimes unsure as to the reasons for an award of a free-kick, the club had suggested to the Football Association that referees should give a signal to indicate whether a free-kick was direct or indirect. 'This is a very good move on the part of Portsmouth, because there are several little points like this and the game would be far more enjoyable if steps were taken to "keep the public informed",' concluded 'Ranger' in his editorial in the *Football Mail* of 28 February.

The team got back on track with a 2-0 home win over bottom of the table Birmingham City, which cut the gap over new leaders Manchester United to just four points. Injuries had again eaten into Jackson's squad, so to lead the attack he was forced to call up 18-year-old Royal Marine Peter Higham, who had just a handful of reserve outings behind him. Only the defiance of Gil Merrick in the Birmingham goal kept the score down, but it took a last-minute goal from Harris to kill off any hope Birmingham nurtured of an unlikely point.

The club entered March with 36 points from thirty games. It was looking increasingly likely that a relatively low points total would secure the championship. At the corresponding point of the previous season Pompey had six more points and led the table by four. Following the Birmingham game the top of the table looked like this:

	P	Pts		P	Pts
1. Manchester U	30	40	5. Blackpool	29	36
2. Liverpool	30	40	6. Arsenal	31	36
3. Sunderland	30	37	7. Wolves	30	36
4. Portsmouth	30	36			

With so many teams jostling for position, and so many having to face one another, it was dog eat dog with plenty of points scattered in the process. From Pompey's point of view it was vital they put February's setbacks behind them, starting with the rearranged midweek trip to Derby County, originally scheduled for FA Cup fifth round day. The team hoped to re-launch their title push. Instead they would find themselves embroiled in a controversy whose ramifications would rumble on until the end of the season.

League Championship celebration dinner, held at Southsea (August 1949)

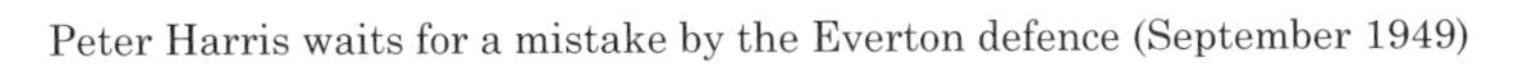

Peter Harris waits for a mistake by the Everton defence (September 1949)

Ike Clarke shoots against Bolton, but keeper Hanson has it covered (Sept 1949)

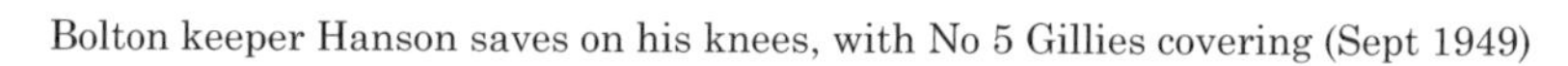
Bolton keeper Hanson saves on his knees, with No 5 Gillies covering (Sept 1949)

Pompey goalie Ernie Butler clears at Manchester United (April 1950)

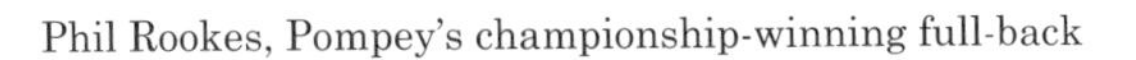

Phil Rookes, Pompey's championship-winning full-back

Peter Harris, Pompey's flying international winger

Pompey directors, officials and players with the English Championship trophy

8

Fight to the Finish

March 1950 – May 1950

Derby went into the crucial match at the Baseball Ground against Pompey on 8 March deflated by a 1-2 home defeat by lowly Everton in the quarter-finals of the FA Cup. The setback affected local support to such an extent that the Wednesday afternoon fixture attracted a crowd of fewer than 18,000, well below Derby's average home gate. But at the conclusion of a tempestuous ninety minutes, Pompey's championship-retaining dream looked dead. Added to which, the club suffered the ignominy of Jimmy Scoular being sent off, along with Derby's Johnny Morris, for an off-the-ball scuffle. Not many spectators saw the incident in which Scoular allegedly kicked out at Morris, upon which the Derby man laid Scoular out with his fist. Morris walked at once, but Scoular had to be helped from the pitch by the trainer. Only later did the referee confirm that both men had been officially expelled.

Younger readers familiar only with the epidemic of red cards that litters the modern game might not appreciate that in former times sending a player off was so uncommon that it was tantamount to a badge of everlasting shame. Even cautions were rare. Seasons could pass between one booking and the next, and decades between sendings off. It is for this reason that to describe a bygone player as never having been booked or sent off in his career is such an empty compliment, for it was nigh impossible to enter the referee's black book for any offence whatsoever. To be sent off half a century ago was an act sure to make headlines in the following day's sports pages. There seems little doubt that in those times players generally acted with greater restraint and showed more respect for the word of the officials, yet it would be worthwhile seeing how a spiky character like Scoular would have fared by the standards applied in the modern game.

Scoular had a reputation for being dour – similar to Reid in the respect that he used his words sparingly – but off the field he was generous towards those he regarded as close friends. On the field he had a fiery temper and a ferocious tackle – 'the finest tackler I ever saw', according to the late Duncan Edwards of Manchester United fame – which made him the man that opposing crowds loved to hate. However, there was more to his game than putting his stocky, muscular frame to destructive use. He could also pass the ball superbly, picking out Harris and Froggatt with pinpoint precision, and he would represent his native Scotland on nine occasions. His scowling features were crowned by a bush of wavy hair but, curiously, for one so fearsome, his idea of relaxation was to take part in crown green bowling tournaments. His father, who represented Scotland at the sport, would come down to the south coast during the summer, and father and son would head off to participate in some of the major tournaments.

Scoular's dismissal at Derby meant he would have to await the FA's deliberations on a suitable punishment – automatic suspensions for cautions and dismissals were still several years away – and the FA's next disciplinary meeting wasn't scheduled for several weeks. In the short term, Pompey were probably more aggrieved to have dropped two more points, especially as Reg Pickett had given them a first-half lead. But Derby rallied and two goals from Jackie Stamps – the winner when he shoulder-charged Butler into the net – gave them the win. 'Ranger' singled out stand-in centre-half Bill Thompson for particular criticism and concluded: 'There have been quite a lot of rumours recently about Pompey players asking to be put on the transfer list, but I believe all these little difficulties, mostly from misunderstanding have been smoothed out. After Wednesday's display some of the players might get a shock if they renewed their applications. They might be granted.'

By the following Saturday the Portsmouth public appeared to be resigned to the worst, for fewer than 27,000 turned up for the visit of mid-table Burnley, who hadn't won a game since Christmas Eve. Buoyed by an early goal, gifted by former Pompey keeper Jimmy Strong, two points were collected in a 2-1 win, but with Manchester United recovering from 0-2 down at Middlesbrough to win 3-2, the gap between fifth-placed Pompey and the leaders remained six points. 'If United can manage to hold their own between now and May 6, the championship will be theirs,' was 'Ranger's' pessimistic view.

Pompey's prospects were seemingly dealt another blow on the Friday prior to the trip to Sunderland. Froggatt had twisted his knee, which had been troubling him for weeks, and an initial diagnosis meant a cartilage operation – which would rule him out for the rest of the season. Despite this unwelcome news, Pompey steered clear of the transfer market before deadline day, enabling young winger Ron Bennett to step up from the reserves to make his second first-team appearance. Fourth-placed Sunderland had made a blind-side run for the title, having taken fourteen points out of the last sixteen. They also remained unbeaten at home. However,

Pompey pinched a goal through Bennett, and though Davis levelled three minutes later, a point was a good return. The *Football Mail* carried a wired picture of the action from Roker Park in that evening's edition, thanks to the fact the *Sunderland Echo* was a sister paper, owned by the same company – Portsmouth & Sunderland Newspapers. Following the game Dickinson stayed up in the north-east, having been selected to represent the Football League against their Scottish counterparts at Middlesbrough on the Wednesday.

The Football League won 3-1 and Pompey received welcome news when Froggatt returned from seeing a surgeon in Newcastle. On examining the knee, he decided that the injury did not require an operation. Froggatt resumed his place on the wing for the visit of Chelsea, who were still smarting from their midweek FA Cup semi-final replay defeat by Arsenal. The Pensioners' hangover was not eased by Reid heading a hat-trick in Pompey's 4-0 win. With Manchester United going down 1-3 at Huddersfield, the gap was now four points. Crucially Pompey had a match in hand – and the leaders still to play at Old Trafford in April. Hope sprung eternal. 'This football can win Championship' ran the *Evening News* headline of the Chelsea match report on the Monday.

The stakes mounted the following week as Pompey teased out a 1-0 win at Stoke. The points were secured by Harris's fierce shot after half-time, and despite Flewin having to leave the field shortly afterwards with a cut head, returning only for the last twenty minutes. The significance of that win was underlined when other scores filtered through. Manchester United only drew 1-1 with Everton, while Blackpool drew 0-0 at Derby. United remained top with 46 points, one point ahead of FA Cup finalists Liverpool, 1-0 home winners over Charlton. Pompey remained fifth, three points short of the leaders. With seven games to go, a photo finish now seemed assured.

Fulham were Good Friday's visitors to Fratton Park, where Harris exhibited his repertoire of skills. He was doubtless frustrated by the international selectors' decision to overlook him for England's crucial Home International match at Hampden the following Saturday, which doubled as a clinching World Cup qualifier for the finals in Brazil. Though Dickinson had been named in England's eleven, that meant he would miss the vital match at Old Trafford. In those times international matches were customarily played on the same day as League fixtures, with the national XI having first call on a player's services. Poor Cottagers' full-back Joe Bacuzzi was left bemused and bewildered by Harris's pace and trickery. Harris put Pompey one-up after seventeen minutes, then lobbed the second after the break. For good measure he manufactured the third for Froggatt to head home. Once again results elsewhere smiled on Pompey. Manchester United lost at home to struggling Birmingham, while Blackpool were slipping off the pace, losing 0-3 at Everton. Liverpool took over at the top with a 2-0 win at Burnley and now seemed in pole position, with the 'double' which had eluded Pompey the year before tantalisingly close to the Anfield club. Six teams still harboured realistic hopes of the title, however, as a glance at the table following the fixtures on Friday, 7 April showed:

	P	Pts		P	Pts
1. Liverpool	37	47	4. Portsmouth	36	45
2. Manchester U	37	46	5. Blackpool	35	44
3. Sunderland	37	46	6. Wolves	35	43

Suddenly, it was Portsmouth's turn to suffer the urge to self-destruct. West Brom arrived at Fratton on Easter Saturday struggling to avoid an immediate return to the Second Division from where they had just emerged. Manager Jackson had promised after the Fulham game that the team were 'really going to have a go' at the title. On a blustery afternoon, Albion's rugged approach didn't win them many friends, but it did gain them the points. Left-half Reg Ryan's wind-assisted 35-yarder flew in with a quarter of an hour to play. 'Ranger' arrived at his desk on Monday morning to find the following letter from a fan, post-marked 6pm Saturday, a tribute to the Post Office's efficiency over the Easter weekend. The letter writer had no doubts why Pompey looked set to pack up the championship trophy, ready to be returned to the Football League's headquarters in Preston. The missive read: 'I think it was the bad refereeing. In the first half today [against West Brom] Pompey should have been awarded three penalties. Many will say I am prejudiced. Pompey lost so I should take it like a sportsman ... but the more games I see the more I am convinced, that it is time we had professional referees and linesmen.' *Plus ça change.*

Pompey went into the Easter Monday return at Fulham with their hopes seemingly in tatters. But by the end of the afternoon they were burning brightly once more. The initiative had swung towards Sunderland on the Saturday, as they thrashed Fulham 3-0 at the same venue, while Liverpool were being thumped 1-5 at Newcastle. With Sunderland having a game in hand, the Easter Monday edition of the *Daily Express* had the Roker Park club as 'odds on' to secure their first League title since 1936. Not that it seemed to worry Pompey, who, with a gale-force wind at their backs, tore into Fulham from the first whistle. Ferrier missed a penalty – only the second one he'd taken in his career – after eight minutes, but Clarke put Pompey ahead with an angled shot after Froggatt and Pickett had exchanged passes. The defence withstood a battering in the second half as Fulham took advantage of the gale, but Pompey held firm. When they reached the dressing room they were greeted by a handpicked set of results. Sunderland had lost 0-2 at Middlesbrough, Liverpool 0-1 at home to Burnley, Blackpool 0-1 at home to Everton, Wolves 1-2 at Manchester City. Manchester United could only draw 0-0 at struggling Birmingham. That point carried United back to the top of the table, but it also potentially opened the door for Portsmouth. The following week the two clubs were due to meet at Old Trafford. At kick-off the situation couldn't have been tighter:

	P	Pts		P	Pts
1. Manchester U	39	48	4. Liverpool	39	47
2. Sunderland	38	48	5. Blackpool	37	46
3. Portsmouth	38	47	6. Wolves	37	44

The Scotland versus England international at Hampden Park rendered Dickinson unavailable, his place going to Thompson, but United too were deprived of the services of full-back John Aston. United sprung a surprise, naming 16-year-old office boy Jeffrey Whitefoot at right-half. Pompey recalled Reid and Phillips after injuries had ruled them out of the Easter Monday win at Fulham. Pickett and Delapenha stood down, in what was truly a crunch match for each team's respective title hopes. As the players trotted out 'Ranger' noted in his running report back to the *Football Mail* office in Stanhope Road that the Pompey Supporters' Club banner – with around two dozen fans who had made the journey clustered around it – was in its usual place on the terraces. Jasper Yeuell, recalling events in 1992, spoke fondly of the loyalty of the Pompey fans. 'Many would wait up to 2am for the coach or train returning home from the North after an away match to speak to us and give us a cheer. The Supporters' Club flag was always facing the tunnel at away grounds too. That gave marvellous encouragement.'

That evening, any fans waiting up for the team's return home would know that Pompey now held the whip hand. Despite having to defend for long spells, the team had held out and stole a march on their rivals by scoring twice in the last ten minutes. *Sunday Express* reporter John Wadham hailed Pompey's achievement the following day, reckoning they now had an '18-carat' chance of clinching the title. But he refused to blame United's defeat on the inclusion of young Whitefoot: 'Any attempts to trace Manchester United's downfall to Jeffrey Whitefoot, the 16-year-old boy who turned out for them at right-half, would be unsporting and untrue.

He has the makings of a fine footballer.' Wadham added that the door had been further wrenched open for Pompey by the heroics of Manchester City's German goalkeeper Bert Trautmann, who saved a Sunderland penalty in relegation-threatened City's 2-1 shock win at Roker Park. That result enabled Pompey to claim the lead with just three matches to go.

At Hampden Park, Dickinson was able to 'toast' a double celebration. He had played his part in England's 1-0 win over Scotland, which decided the British Championship. The result had another, altogether more curious downside for the Scotland team. FIFA, in the process of organising the forthcoming World Cup in Brazil that summer, had invited the home countries to send two representatives to the tournament, but in an astonishing display of pig-headness the Scottish FA chose only to accept the invitation should they be British champions. Roy Bentley's second-half goal put paid to that hope, but despite pleas from the SFA president John Lamb and the players, the Scots stood their ground and only England travelled to South America. There they would be humbled by the United States in one of football's all-time upsets.

Dickinson was back on club duty as FA Cup finalists Liverpool descended on Fratton Park needing a win to keep alive their hopes of the double. On their journey to Portsmouth on the Friday, the Liverpool team had taken a detour via Wembley to enable the players to get a feel for the stadium which they would grace in opposition to Arsenal the following week. Liverpool also used the Pompey fixture to air their new Wembley kit, white shirts with red collars and cuffs and black shorts. The Pompey team was unchanged, save for Dickinson's inclusion ahead of Thompson, while Spence continued to deputise for Flewin, who had yet to recover from an eye injury sustained at Stoke three weeks previously. Not surprisingly the match attracted enormous attention, with the ground attendance record possibly under threat. The earliest supporters started queuing at breakfast time and the Portsmouth branch of the Women's League of Health and Beauty rewarded early comers with a pre-match exhibition. Sadly the report does not specify precisely what form this display took, but Phil Rookes recalls that they were usually dressed in white tops and (long) skirts and performed rhythmic exercises and dances to music.

After a cagey first half, first blood went to the visitors when the limping Hindmarsh failed to block Liddell, whose third attempt on goal was deflected in by Stubbins. Butler only narrowly failed to stop the ball crossing the line. The goal served to galvanise Pompey and, urged on by 'chiming' terraces, they hit back nine minutes later. Harris encouraged Minshull to foul him just outside the area, took the free-kick himself, and Reid soared highest to head home.

With tension mounting, Liverpool, who knew defeat would end their double hopes, held out until ten minutes from time. It was then that Scoular, out on the touchline, swung a ball into the area and Froggatt directed a header into the net. The crowd, which was some 4,000 short of the gate record, went wild. 'Ranger' noted that 'This goal ... was greeted with terrific cheering by the crowd which was kept up for several minutes after the game had resumed.' The dying minutes were marked by controversy when Liverpool centre-half Hughes tugged Clarke's shirt to prevent him breaking clear, earning him the crowd's but not the referee's censure.

In his *Sunday Express* report, Alan Hoby divulged that Arsenal had their scout Len Thompson at the game checking up on Liverpool, but that his praise was reserved for the home side: 'Pompey? One word describes them – magnificent, every man of them. No wonder the crowd, 47,500 of them, went delirious when they ran off the field,' he wrote. The title was now a four-horse race. Manchester United were out of the reckoning after their 1-2 setback at Newcastle, but Wolves, Blackpool and Sunderland still nursed ambitions of catching Pompey, who still had to play at Cup finalists Arsenal, and Highbury had never been one of Pompey's happiest hunting grounds. The situation at the top on the evening of 23 April 1950 looked as follows:

	P	Pts		P	Pts
1. Portsmouth	40	51	4. Manchester U	41	48
2. Wolves	40	49	5. Sunderland	40	48
3. Blackpool	39	48	6. Liverpool	41	48

Put simply, two wins from their two outstanding fixtures would guarantee that Pompey retained their crown. The players now had a ten-day break before their next match, with Arsenal. The original fixture was scheduled for Saturday, 30 April, but the Gunners were otherwise engaged with the Cup final. On the same day, Wolves drew level on points, recovering from a two-goal deficit at Bolton to win 4-2. Sunderland maintained their outside interest with a home win over Everton by the same score. Blackpool's challenge seemed to be fading, however. In midweek they lost their game in hand, going down 0-1 at West Brom, and then managed only a draw at Stoke. The mathematics were clear. One win from their final two matches would deliver the title to Fratton Park for a second time in a row, as Pompey had a vastly superior goal-average over any of their rivals.

Goal-average had come to Portsmouth's aid in the past. In May 1927, second-placed Pompey were level on points with Manchester City going into the final round of matches in the Second Division.

It had been a two-horse race for the second promotion spot, with Pompey holding a slender goal-average advantage over their rivals. Pompey's home fixture with Preston kicked off fifteen minutes after City's game with Bradford at Maine Road. With ten minutes left Pompey led 4-1, but the crowd's confidence was shattered as word filtered from the press box – which had put through a telephone call to Manchester to establish the final result – and learned that City had thrashed Bradford 8-0. Frantic pencil and paper calculations revealed Pompey needed one more goal to ensure their place in Division One for the first time. Billy 'Farmer's Boy' Haines duly obliged with his fourth of the game and fortieth of the season, sparking ecstatic scenes at the end of the match. Pompey had secured their elevation by 1/200th part of a goal, the narrowest goal-average margin ever to secure a promotion in the Football League.

If that occasion was anything to go by, Pompey were more than capable of holding their nerve, if need be. However, they had a shock in store from a surprise quarter. The Football Association chose this inopportune moment to announce their disciplinary decision regarding the sending off of Scoular at Derby back in March. On Friday, 29 April the FA announced that the player would be suspended for fourteen days from 1 May, ruling him out of the final two matches against Arsenal and Aston Villa. The club and, in particular the supporters, were incensed that it should have taken so long to decide the punishment. Writing to the *Evening News*, one supporter, who hailed from Stubbington, near Fareham, summed up the mood: 'I am not concerned at the moment with Scoular and it is conceivable that the club should be made to feel its responsibility in this matter, but why, in the name of justice, must the anything from the two to 20,000 of us who will be at Highbury tomorrow be punished also? No doubt the FA committee are strictly impartial and in their saintly innocence will not realise they should not only avoid evil but also the appearance of evil. This they have not done, in fact many thousands of football supporters (not all of them from this district either) will regard their latest action as savouring of a carefully timed discriminatory action against the Portsmouth club and a callous disregard of the welfare of the football going public.'

Fate conspired to deal the team further blows on the eve of the game against Arsenal, who were celebrating their 2-0 FA Cup final win over Liverpool and decided to play Pompey in the same yellow jerseys they had worn at Wembley. Flewin's anticipated return was put on hold as his eye had not responded to treatment. Spence kept his place, but then it was learned that Clarke was out, requiring an operation on an injured toe. The ever-willing Thompson filled in at right-half, while Pickett came in for Clarke. For Arsenal, Joe Mercer and Denis Compton were both bidding farewell to the club. The gates closed long before kick-off with more than 63,000 inside Highbury. The crowd were entertained by a girl pipers' band, a military band and, according to Desmond Hackett's account in the *Daily Express*, 'lots of be-tartaned girls walking round with the Cup and looking quite bewildered.' Clearly, pre-match entertainment these days is not what it was.

Once play commenced, Portsmouth spurned the chance of an early goal. Reid and Pickett dithered over the opportunity and Leslie Compton cleared. Goring took advantage shortly afterwards, nodding home Denis Compton's corner in the 25th minute. Despite retaliating bravely, Pompey could not get back on terms. Froggatt was inches from getting his head to a Pickett centre in the second half and Arsenal wrapped up the points with ten minutes to go. Logie put Goring in the clear to fire past Butler and record his second goal of the game. Afterwards, 'Ranger' claimed Pompey had had enough of the ball to gain a point, but 'fiddled' too much, but it was clear the supporters' hopes were still high as hundreds of them surrounded the team bus before it departed to give the players a rousing send-off.

Denmark, of all places, kept a keen eye on Pompey's progress. Witness this icy comment by 'Ranger': 'Portsmouth's ... fight to retain the League Championship Cup may not have been welcomed with big headlines in London newspapers, but it appealed to the sporting public of Denmark where Pompey's performance was heralded in large type.' What with the Scoular affair and a lack of recognition in the national press, it seemed the Portsmouth sporting public had a collective chip on its shoulder.

However, the destiny of the title still remained in Pompey's own hands. Lowly Aston Villa were due at Fratton for the final game of the season, while second-placed Wolves entertained a similarly troubled Birmingham City, but Pompey's overwhelming goal-tally meant that barring the proverbial divine intervention a win would be enough. The fly in the ointment was Sunderland, who could pip both leading clubs by winning while they both lost. The Rokermen were at home to Chelsea.

Jackson had to re-jig his team once more, pushing utility man Thompson to lead the attack for the first time in his professional career. Thompson replaced the injured Pickett, Spence moved to right-half to cover for the suspended Scoular, and Flewin returned at centre-half.

From the moment Thompson marked his centre-forward 'debut' with a goal after twenty seconds – latching onto Froggatt's through pass – the destiny of the League Championship was never in doubt.

At half-time Pompey led 2-0, after which the crowd could afford the luxury of greeting regular updates of Wolves' 6-1 winning score with ironic cheers. Pompey ended up thrashing Villa 5-1 (Villa's goal coming at 5-0, when it counted for nothing), with Reid helping himself to a hat-trick. The crowd avalanched onto the pitch at the final whistle for the second time in a little over twelve months, saluting the men who had turned Portsmouth FC into the best team in the country. Although it could never be put to the competitive test in those days, Pompey were possibly the best in Europe too.

This was the first League title to be determined by goal-average for 26 years, but the final margin was a whopping – in arithmetical terms at least – four tenths of a goal. In retrospect, Wolves had needed twenty goals in their last match to overtake Pompey's goal-figures. The runners-up spot in Division Two was also decided by goal-average, with three teams finishing on 52 points. Sheffield Wednesday pipped city rivals United by 0.008 of a goal. Southampton, who narrowly missed out on promotion for the second successive season, were a further fraction behind.

Portsmouth's joy in securing successive championships was such that the club and its supporters could forgive Alex James' bizarre choice of teams of the year in the *Daily Express*. Despite becoming the first side to retain the title since Arsenal in 1935, his 'team of the year' was Second Division champions Tottenham, with Cup-winners Arsenal only slightly less deserving. 'Don't think I'm knocking Pompey,' he blushed, 'it takes a wonderful side to win the league championship two years running.' Reading between the lines, James evidently considered it was more 'wonderful' to win the Second Division once than to win the First twice!

Immediately after the Aston Villa match, win or lose, the players were booked to take an open-topped bus to the Guildhall and enjoy a dinner-dance in their honour. Staff preparing the banquet-hall anxiously awaited news from Fratton Park before putting the finishing touches to the menu with a hastily added cartoon. As Pompey were victorious, it featured a caricature of a rival player snatching the trophy away, with a Pompey player shouting 'Oi! Put that back'. Had Pompey lost, the caption would have been switched to read 'Don't pack it. Polish it!' Hundreds of fans thronged the Guildhall Square to cheer the team, and a handful hung on until midnight to applaud them as they left.

Cllr Frank Miles, the city's deputy mayor, summed up the mood of everyone: 'I can't think of a greater asset for the city than the famous Portsmouth FC which has not only national, but international fame. There must have been thousands of people in all parts of the world who were interested in what was happening.' Monty, too, added his congratulations with a letter to the chairman, Mr Chinneck, which concluded: 'I somehow knew we would do it.'

Not until Matt Busby's great Manchester United side of 1956 and 1957 would Pompey's feat of successive championships be repeated. That is a measure of Pompey's worth. How sad that the European Champions Cup was but a futuristic dream in 1950. Other national champions that year included Benfica, Juventus, Atletico Madrid. The mouth waters at the prospect of what might have been.

Pompey director Syd Leverett with the championship trophy at the train station

Lindy Delapenha, Pompey's first black footballer

Flat caps, woolly jerseys, and heavy leather balls – football in the 1940s!

Goalmouth action at home to Sunderland. Pompey won 4-1 (October 1946)

Preston's goalie and Doug Reid watch Williams deflect into his own goal (Jan 1948)

Heading clear a soggy leather football would give most people headaches

9

How the Mighty Fell

Post-1950

In May 1950, Portsmouth FC were without peer in the domestic game, yet within a few years the club would become shadows of their former selves, plunging into the Third Division in 1961 and the Fourth in 1978. Their fall from grace provides a salutary tale for provincial clubs everywhere.

If the first half of the twentieth century saw Portsmouth FC on a seemingly inexorable climb towards stardom, it is clear from today's vantage-point that 1950 signalled its high-water mark. The next thirty years would see the club brought to its knees, as, one by one, links with the greatest era in the club's history were severed. The dismantling of Pompey's championship team started even before the 1949-50 season was over, although the initial departures affected the margins rather than the core. With the title still up for grabs in those final cliff-hanging days, Jamaican winger Lindy Delapenha, frustrated by his lack of first-team opportunities, signed for Middlesbrough. Bert Barlow, one of the veterans of 1939, had departed the previous December for Second Division Leicester City. Now, with the championship in the bag, the summons came for players to represent England in the World Cup finals in Brazil. Jimmy Dickinson received the anticipated call-up, but the selection committee turned its back on Froggatt and Harris.

England's was to be a less than glorious World Cup debut – this being the first time they had deigned to enter the competition since its inauguration in 1930 – and despite a 2-0 win over Chile in their opening game, the tournament will be remembered for one result only. On Thursday, 29 June, in the shabby stadium at Belo Horizonte, a mining town 300 miles from Rio de Janeiro, Dickinson took his place in the blue-shirted England team that shockingly lost 0-1 to the part-timers of the USA. Any pretensions about England being the best in the world were shattered forever. Following a further 0-1 defeat against Spain, Dickinson and the rest were on the boat home.

In Pompey terms, that disappointment was nothing compared to the shock still reverberating around Fratton Park. In late May the FA had suspended directors Vernon Stokes and Harry Wain *sine die* from all activities in football. The furore centred on an alleged £750 illegal payment to Jimmy McAlinden, when he had returned to Portsmouth from Ireland after the war. The player – who was by now playing for Southend United – was also suspended, in his case until 1 October. The Pompey Supporters Club was so indignant at what they perceived as an injustice that they agitated for a petition that eventually ran to 25,000 signatures. The FA finally relented in February 1951, rescinding the bans. Stokes was re-elected chairman for the 1951-52 season.

Chasing a third successive title – as predicted by Monty after the first – the team were to find consistency elusive until it was too late. Relying largely on the championship-winning players who had served the club so handsomely, Pompey made an indifferent start – notwithstanding the traditional thrashing of whipping-boys Everton, 5-1 at Goodison Park. A November defeat by the same score at Tottenham, who had, under Arthur Rowe, advanced a 'push and run' style of football in winning the Second Division title, dumped Pompey into the lower half of the table. Spurs would go on to seize Portsmouth's crown, which suggested that times were indeed a-changing. The season's nadir came at Second Division Luton in the FA Cup third round, when Pompey crashed 0-2, leaving them with nothing to play for. Butler's return in goal in February coincided with a run of one defeat in fourteen matches, which endured to the end of the season, but in the final analysis ten home draws did not merit anything higher than seventh place. Pompey's total of 47 points was an unbridgeable thirteen fewer than that earned by the new champions.

A golden era was over, and so were the days of regular 'house full' signs at Fratton Park. Attendances were on the wane across the country and the 49,716 gate for the visit of Tottenham in March 1951 would be the last time the ground record would be remotely threatened. The season's low saw just 22,411 turn up for the December 'black Saturday' game with Huddersfield.

In May 1951 Pompey embarked on a three-week tour of South America, returning winless, but the tour was overshadowed by the sending off of Jimmy Scoular – by English referee Arthur Ellis, who had accompanied the party – in the first match. The 1-2 defeat by the Brazilian side Fluminese, in front of an estimated 200,000 crowd in the Maracana Stadium, set the tone. Pompey returned home with just a couple of draws from five games.

It was during that summer that Pompey finally joined the ranks of big spenders, investing £20,000 in Chesterfield winger Gordon Dale. Championship stalwarts Hindmarsh and Rookes departed for clubs in the Third Division (South) – Hindmarsh for Swindon, and Rookes, who never fully recovered from an ankle injury sustained in the 7-0 FA Cup thrashing of Stockport in January 1949, for Colchester. Rookes' injury effectively put paid to his Pompey career and was especially galling as the initial damage took months to be properly diagnosed. The player recalls: 'Although I was carried off in the Stockport game and taken home by car, the injured ankle (a chipped bone and hairline fracture) was never X-rayed! Only later in a reserve match at Millwall, when I was again injured and carried off, was I sent to hospital. The X-ray then showed up the previous January injuries and a further chipped bone! The club's incompetence ruined my career with them and they ended up having to pay a big fee for Jimmy Stephen.'

Despite another plague of injuries during the winter of 1951-52, it seemed that Pompey might be on the verge of reasserting themselves. In March 1952 they found themselves handily placed in third position, three points behind leaders Manchester United, with a quarter-final home tie against Newcastle in the FA Cup to look forward to. Dreams of the elusive double fleetingly beckoned once more. The Magpies quickly snuffed them out, winning 4-2 on what the eminent *Times* journalist Geoffrey Green described as 'a grey afternoon touched by glory'. *Sunday Express* reporter Alan Hoby headlined his report 'The greatest game I have ever seen.' The team which represented Pompey that afternoon retained a familiar feel, although Froggatt had by now established himself as centre-half in place of Flewin, with Belgian Marcel Gaillard, a signing from Crystal Palace, playing on the wing. The claims of youth could also no longer be denied. A 19-year-old Scottish centre-forward, Jackie Henderson, had ousted Ike Clarke, while Portsmouth-born Phil Gunter, the same age, made the right-back spot his own.

With five League games to play Pompey were just a point off the top, but losing their final four matches put paid to their hopes. Ferrier, Butler, Scoular and Harris all passed the 200-appearance mark for the club, but manager Jackson had called upon 28 players that season, a stark contrast with the eighteen used when winning the League for the first time. Len Phillips made his England debut, but was transfer-listed in January 1952, with Pompey reportedly demanding £30,000 for his services. By the end of the season he had made his peace with the club.

The summer of 1952 saw 'bow-tie Bob' – manager Jackson – surprisingly leave the club to take charge at ambitious Second Division Hull City, but he was fated not to repeat his success in East Yorkshire. The Tigers were relegated under Jackson's stewardship, for which he found himself relieved of his duties. Pompey replaced Jackson with Eddie Lever, the former school-teacher who had for several years been working with the reserves, but the new boss took time to acclimatise in his new role. One of Lever's first tasks was to sell full-back Jasper Yeuell to Barnsley, but the 1952-53 season started disastrously for Pompey – a 0-2 home defeat by Blackpool setting the tone for a campaign which saw the team finish fifteenth, their lowest position since the war. That season also saw goalkeeper Butler fracture his wrist in a reserve game, and in the summer of 1953 it prompted his retirement. Another championship hero on his way that summer was Jimmy Scoular, who moved to Newcastle for £22,500, having been in dispute with Pompey for many months. He had been placed on the transfer list after being dropped in December, but although he regained his place he remained a disgruntled presence at the club. At St James' Park the Scot would captain his new team to FA Cup final glory in 1955 against Manchester City. After he retired as a player, Scoular became manager of Second Division Cardiff City, with whom he crossed swords with Portsmouth several times. He almost took the Welsh club into the First Division in 1971, and masterminded a number of highly-charged European nights at Ninian Park, among them a Cup-Winners' Cup quarter-final with Real Madrid. Cliff Parker also retired in June 1953 at the age of 39.

By now Pompey were not even confident of finishing in the top half of the First Division. A dreadful start to the 1953-54 season – the first four matches were lost – suggested a long struggle against relegation. An unbeaten home run from November to the end of the season eventually killed off the unthinkable, although fourteenth place was far from what the fans had become accustomed to. Their disillusionment was underlined by a sparse crowd of 15,000 for a midweek rearranged game with Sheffield Wednesday in April. At the root of Lever's problems was his inability to field a settled side: injuries of one kind or another forced him to call upon 33 players in competitive fixtures. Inevitably, the prowess of some of the former champions still in the team faded as time and injuries took their toll. Full-back Harry Ferrier, now 34, left the club in the summer of 1954 to become player-manager at Southern League Gloucester City. Some months earlier Jack Froggatt had been sold to Leicester City.

One player who seemed as sprightly as ever was winger Peter Harris, who finished the 1953-54 season leading scorer with twenty goals. These included his 100th for the club in 268 appearances. Harris's form even earned him an England recall – his previous appearance had been in the inglorious 0-2 home defeat by the Republic of Ireland in 1949 – and on 23 May 1954 he duly lined up in the eleven to face Hungary in Budapest. The previous November Dickinson had been in the England team humiliated 6-3 by the magical Magyars at Wembley, a match that stripped away any vestige of national footballing superiority. Now the two teams met again. Could England spring a surprise? The Pompey duo did their best, but that afternoon England lost by the improbable margin of 1-7, and 28-year-old Harris's international career was over. When the squad for the forthcoming World Cup finals in Switzerland was announced, Harris's name was absent, but Dickinson kept his place and participated in another of England's abortive bids to claim the Jules Rimet trophy.

Since signing for Portsmouth back in 1944, Dickinson had been a virtual ever-present, but manager Lever's plans for the 1954-55 season were thrown into doubt when a pre-season injury caused his star left-half to miss the first six games. Dickinson's return lasted only until November, when he broke his ankle in the home match with Cardiff and was out for another four months. Ironically, with the exception of Dickinson, Lever had a settled squad to choose from, and the benefits of continuity were reflected on the field. Despite losing 1-2 at Second Division Bristol Rovers in the FA Cup third round, in the League the team remained in the hunt for the title. Games in hand on leaders Chelsea made their title bid realistic, provided they beat the London club at home on 16 April. More than 40,000 packed Fratton Park for the occasion but Chelsea hung on for a 0-0 draw, after which Pompey's season petered out, ending with a 2-5 collapse at Sheffield United. It would be the last time a Portsmouth team would challenge for the League title.

The links with past glories were by now fast falling apart. Knee problems severely affected Len Phillips' fitness and in September 1956, aged 33, he drew the curtain down on his top-flight career, moving to Southern League Poole Town. By then his inside-forward partner, Duggie Reid, had also retired from the professional game. Age and injuries had finally caught up with the craggy Scot, who was now fast approaching forty. He was a regular at centre-half at the start of the 1955-56 season, before losing his place to Phil Gunter, but was allowed one last 'hurrah' at inside-forward in the final game of that campaign, a 2-4 defeat by Manchester City in April 1956. Reid left to become manager of Southern League Tonbridge, although his Fratton Park connection would shortly be renewed.

That 1955-56 season also saw the death of long-serving director Harry Wain and the first-ever floodlit game in the Football League, when Fratton Park hosted an evening match with Newcastle in February 1956. Although friendly matches had been played under lights for several years, the League had remained sceptical. The public, too, seemed unenthusiastic, with a gate to commemorate the occasion of less than 16,000, well below the average, but history proved the event to be a landmark occasion. Pompey lost the match

0-2 and at the end of the season the team found itself twelfth in the First Division, respectable enough, but there was no doubting the bubble was close to bursting.

Off the field, plans for a new £40,000 two-tier stand on the Fratton End had been drawn up. The structure was in place for the first home game of the 1956-57 season against Sheffield Wednesday. The match was won 3-1, but of the championship side only Dickinson and Harris remained first-team regulars. By the time of the return at Hillsborough in April, Pompey were in dire straits. A 1-3 defeat was the team's fifth in six matches and the result left them in acute danger of relegation. Only an improbable six-point Easter spared them that indignity. Dickinson had demonstrated the selflessness that epitomised his attitude to the game, filling in at Pompey's problem position at centre-half, a decision that seems effectively to have terminated his international career. His final appearance in an England shirt came in the 5-2 win over Denmark in a World Cup qualifying match at Molineux in December 1956.

Manager Eddie Lever was increasingly obliged to scrabble in the lower divisions for players as dwindling gates cut revenues, but it seemed the club's scouting network was still thriving, throwing up a few gems. Young centre-forward Ray Crawford, Portsmouth-born, was emerging through the ranks and in August 1957 Lever announced the signing of another forward, 19-year-old Derek Dougan from Northern Ireland club Distillery. Both youngsters made their mark during the 1957-58 season, scoring vital goals as Pompey somehow avoided the drop, this time by the wafer-thin margin of goal-average.

That miserable season cost Lever his job, but this time there was no natural successor waiting in the wings. The Pompey board instead looked along the coast to Bournemouth, where Freddie Cox had guided the Third Division (South) side to the quarter-finals of the 1958 FA Cup. Cox's apparent ability to turn sows' ears into silk purses on a shoestring seduced an increasingly cash-conscious board, and in the summer of 1958 he set about his new task with relish. However, it was soon apparent that his uncompromising style – not to mention tactics – was making him few friends in the dressing room. By December 1958 the promising Crawford had departed for Ipswich, where he would win a League championship medal and play for England, and three months later Dougan was allowed to sign for Blackburn. In due course Dougan would enjoy a colourful career in the top flight with Wolves, and would represent Northern Ireland. Another Portsmouth-born forward, Johnny Gordon, was sold to Birmingham as Cox set about trying to confirm his theory that lower division sweat could take the place of First Division style.

It was a policy doomed to failure. The only highlights of a catastrophic 1958-59 season saw Jimmy Dickinson celebrate his 500th appearance in a 4-4 draw at Tottenham in February and Peter Harris set a record for a winger by netting all five goals in the 5-2 home win over Aston Villa in September. These were tiny rays of light in a season of unfathomable darkness. The team did not win after November and signed off the season with nine straight losses. Dickinson and Harris were powerless to prevent relegation, nine years after they had helped retain the championship in that dramatic finale against Aston Villa. The crowd of 14,000 for the final home game of 1958-59 was barely a quarter of that which had witnessed the Villa extravaganza.

If supporters thought a spell in the Second Division would assist the club to consolidate, they were sorely mistaken. Harris was compelled to stop playing in the autumn of 1959, victim of a serious chest complaint, but enjoyed a testimonial match that rekindled fading championship memories. Meanwhile, dire displays on the pitch saw gates tumble below 10,000 for the first time since the war. In August 1960 Pompey's last ties with the championship team were 35-year-old Dickinson, Reg Flewin, who was the club's assistant manager, chief scout Bill Thompson, and Reid, who had returned in the summer of 1958 as groundsman at the club's Tamworth Road training ground. Reid also ran a hostel for the club's young players. The third game of 1960-61 saw newly promoted Southampton thrash Pompey 5-1 at the Dell. Another long, hard winter beckoned and the axis of southern football had begun to shift. The gloomy portents were not misplaced. Cox was sacked in February 1961 with Pompey in the relegation frame.

By this time Harris had retired and Flewin had departed to try his luck as manager at Third Division Stockport. The board named Thompson as caretaker boss while a successor was sought, but Thompson could do little to arrest a side in free-fall. When George Smith was named as Cox's successor in April 1961, not even a run of six points from the last ten could prevent the club slipping into the Third Division for the first time since 1924.

The appointment of the disciplinarian Smith actually prolonged Dickinson's career. The new manager restored Dickinson to the captaincy – he had been 'too old for the job' according to Cox – and played him in his proper position, left-half. In September 1961, against Barnsley at Fratton, Dickinson played his 600th League match. Promotion followed in the spring, but the football world had fundamentally changed. The maximum wage had been abolished the previous year and when Fulham became the first club to pay a player – Johnny Haynes – £100 per week, the game embarked on an inflationary spiral that shows few signs of abating. In many ways Pompey could consider themselves unfortunate to have lost their top-flight status when they did. It is noteworthy that the likes of Huddersfield and Cardiff – whose experiences mirror Pompey's in the final quarter of the twentieth century – were also cast out of the First Division in the late 1950s. By the time these clubs had readjusted to a football world where financial muscle shaped the order of things, past success counted for nothing. The new football ethos was one in which a man like Dickinson could never be totally at ease. In the summer of 1964, having learned that he was to receive an MBE for services to Association Football, he announced that he was embarking on his final season.

And Jim had one last playing service to perform for his club. On Easter Monday 1965 he made his final League appearance at Fratton Park, with his beloved club hovering on the brink of the Third Division. Almost 16,000, well above average, turned out for the occasion and Pompey responded with a 4-0 win over Norwich that gave them a fighting chance of staying up. 'Gentleman Jim' – the sobriquet derives from his having played 764 League games without ever incurring a caution – was rested for the return at Carrow Road, which Pompey lost 1-3. Dickinson's last ever game was at Northampton with Pompey needing a draw on this, the final day of the season, to avert the drop. A late equaliser by veteran full-back Alex Wilson, who had signed for Pompey from Scottish junior football back in 1949, did the trick and Dickinson was shouldered from the field by players and fans.

Smith had already promised him a coaching job, but Dickinson insisted that route was not for him, modern-day football becoming an increasing anathema to him. Instead he became the club's first public relations officer. With Reid now promoted to head groundsman, the club retained two links with the championship years. But Dickinson, who became club secretary in 1968, and Reid were forced to see their club almost brought to its knees. The reserve and youth teams had been scrapped, and the fifty professionals on the books in 1949 were now reduced to a first-team squad of just seventeen.

By the mid-1970s the financial situation was so desperate that unless £25,000 was raised Portsmouth Football Club was faced with bankruptcy. That crisis was averted, with Dickinson playing his part, helping to organise fund-raising schemes, such as sponsoring Reid's immaculately maintained Fratton turf by the square foot. Managers came and went. In May 1977, when the latest, Ian St John, was shown the door, Dickinson was persuaded that only he could save 'his' team from further relegation. As caretaker boss he secured a point at Preston in his first match and masterminded a 3-1 win at Fratton over doomed York to ensure Pompey's safety.

In the emotionally charged aftermath Dickinson was seduced into becoming Pompey's ninth post-war manager. It was an unwise decision on everyone's part. A year later his inability to impose his 1950s perspective on the modern world played its part in the club tumbling into Division Four. Dickinson sacrificed that which is most precious of all, his health, to the only professional club he had ever known. In March 1979 he suffered a heart attack at Barnsley and was hospitalised for weeks. His reign as manager was over.

Dickinson was assured of a job at Fratton Park for life and in 1979-80 he returned as 'chief executive', a title which indicated the esteem in which the club held him. His duties were light, for he was still poorly. He attended Duggie Reid's testimonial (Reid had retired in 1978) against Southampton in May 1980, and lined up with his championship mates for a team picture before the start. It would be his last public appearance with the men who had given Portsmouth FC a greatness not given to many. On 2 November 1982 Dickinson took his seat to watch the 4-1 win over Lincoln, but it would be the last time Fratton saw him. Six days later another heart attack claimed his life at the age of 57. The last link between Portsmouth FC and the Champions of England had gone.

Match programme of the Charity Shield against FA Cup winners Wolves

Doug Reid challenges Wolves keeper Bert Williams (April 1949)

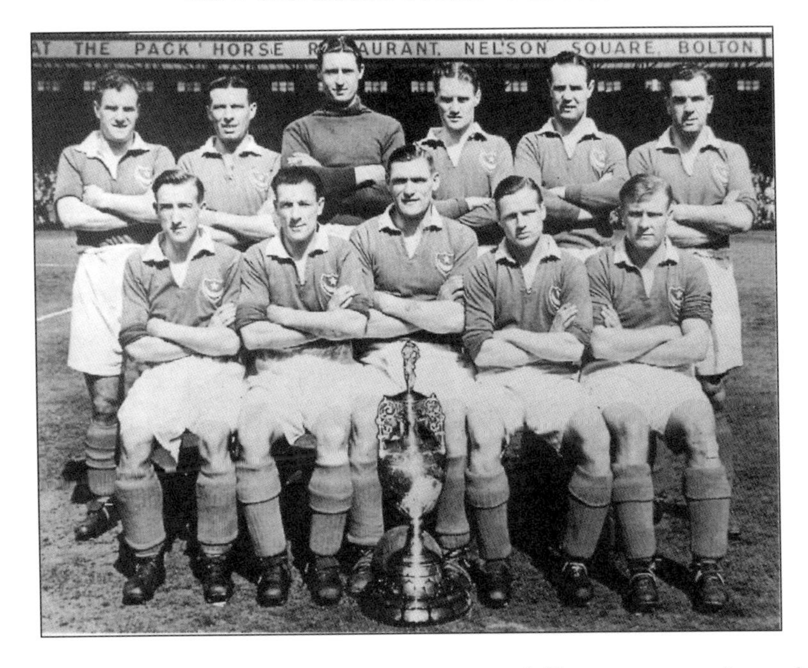

This was taken before the championship was secured. The cup was superimposed

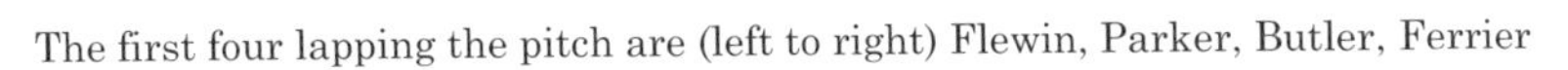
The first four lapping the pitch are (left to right) Flewin, Parker, Butler, Ferrier

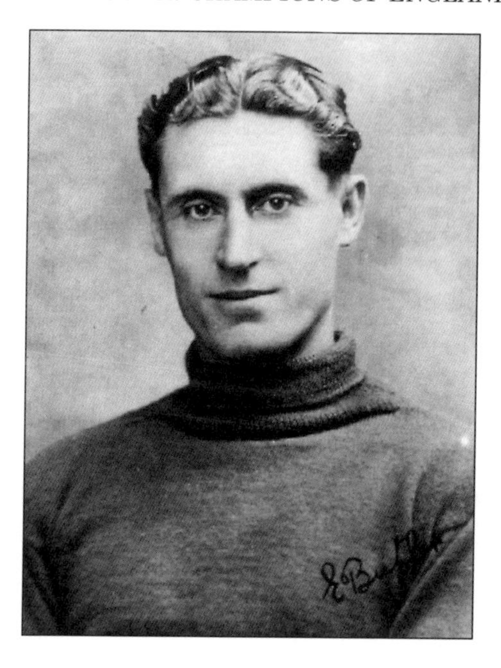

Goalie Ernie Butler played 240 games for Pompey and kept 82 clean sheets

Flewin introduces Montgomery to the champions. Butler shakes his hand

Guide to Seasonal Summaries

Col 1: Match number (for league fixtures); Round (for cup-ties).
e.g. 2:1 means 'Second round; first leg.'
e.g. 4R means 'Fourth round replay.'

Col 2: Date of the fixture and whether Home (H), Away (A), or Neutral (N).

Col 3: Opposition.

Col 4: Attendances. Home gates appear in roman; Away gates in *italics*.
Figures in **bold** indicate the largest and smallest gates, at home and away.
Average home and away attendances appear after the final league match.

Col 5: Respective league positions of Pompey and their opponents after the match.
Pompey's position appears on the top line in roman.
Their opponents' position appears on the second line in *italics*.
For cup-ties, the division and position of opponents is provided.
e.g. *2:12* means the opposition are twelfth in Division 2.

Col 6: The top line shows the result: W(in), D(raw), or L(ose).
The second line shows Pompey's cumulative points total.

Col 7: The match score, Pompey's given first.
Scores in **bold** indicate Pompey's biggest league win and heaviest defeat.

Col 8: The half-time score, Pompey's given first.

Col 9: The top line shows Pompey's scorers and times of goals in roman.
The second line shows opponents' scorers and times of goals in *italics*.
A 'p' after the time of a goal denotes a penalty; 'og' an own-goal.
The third line gives the name of the match referee.

Team line-ups: Pompey line-ups appear on the top line, irrespective of whether they are home or away. Opposition teams appear on the second line in *italics*.
Players of either side who are sent off are marked !
Pompey players making their league debuts are displayed in **bold**.

Substitutes: Names of substitutes appear only if they actually took the field.
A player substituted is marked *
A second player substituted is marked ^
A third player substituted is marked "
These marks do not indicate the sequence of substitutions.

N.B. For clarity, all information appearing in *italics* relates to opposing teams.

LEAGUE DIVISION 1								Manager: Bob Jackson									SEASON 1948-49		
No	Date		Att	Pos	Pt	F-A	H-T	Scorers, Times, and Referees	1	2	3	4	5	6	7	8	9	10	11
1	A	PRESTON			D	2-2	0-1	Reid 63, Barlow 74	Butler	Rookes	Ferrier	Scoular	Flewin	Dickinson	Harris	Reid	Froggatt	Phillips	Barlow
	21/8		*37,062*		1			*Dougal 44, Finney 53p*	*Gooch*	*Walton*	*Scott*	*Horton*	*Corbett*	*Davie*	*Finney*	*Dougal*	*McIntosh*	*Beattie*	*Langton*
								Ref: L Brown (Barnes)	Pompey come from 0-2 down in the drizzle to keep a 23-year unbeaten record at Deepdale. Finney's wing trickery lets him cross for the first, then the 'plumber' is felled in the box by Scoular. Reid nods home Froggatt's cross to set up Barlow's saver. Pompey finish much the stronger.										
2	H	EVERTON			W	4-0	2-0	Froggatt 37, 44, Barlow 56, 83	Butler	Rookes	Ferrier	Scoular	Flewin	Dickinson	Harris	Barlow	Reid	Phillips	Froggatt
	25/8		31,433		3				*Sagar*	*Saunders*	*Drysdale*	*Lindley*	*Jones*	*Farrell*	*McIlhatton*	*Powell*	*Dodds*	*Fielding*	*Eglington*
								Ref: G Clark (London)	Sagar is Everton's saviour as Pompey muff chance after chance. Everton, with Lindley hobbling, finally crack after Froggatt's rocket, which would have beaten any goalkeeper. He then nods home Scoular's cross. An offside denies him a hat-trick, but Barlow's drives seal the points.										
3	H	BURNLEY		2	W	1-0	1-0	Froggatt 15	Butler	Rookes	Ferrier	Scoular	Flewin	Dickinson	Harris	Barlow	Reid	Phillips	Froggatt
	28/8		37,846	*17*	5				*Strong*	*Woodruff*	*Mather*	*Attwell*	*Brown*	*Bray*	*Chew*	*Morris*	*Billingham*	*Potts*	*Wilson*
								Ref: J Tregallas (Birmingham)	Unchanged Pompey resist a second-half barrage at a sultry Fratton. Froggatt is fouled and exacts revenge nodding home Dickinson's free-kick. Wilson misses a sitter for Clarets, letting Butler clear the danger. Reserve Juliussen could be off to Everton, but the directors are tight-lipped.										
4	A	EVERTON		1	W	**5-0**	3-0	Harris 4, Froggatt 35, 40, Reid 52, [Barlow 86]	Butler	Rookes	Ferrier	Scoular	Bowler	Dickinson	Harris	Barlow	Reid	Phillips	Froggatt
	1/9		*41,511*	*22*	7				*Sagar*	*Saunders*	*Drysdale*	*Grant*	*Cameron*	*Farrell*	*McIlhatton*	*Wainwright*	*Dodds*	*Lello*	*McCormack*
								Ref: G Clark (London)	Poor Everton are swamped again as Pompey go top, but it might have been different had Dodds not blazed over just after Froggatt's head made it 2-0. Moments later Sagar misjudges Froggatt's centre and it's all over. Harris (cross-shot) and Reid (header) put Pompey on easy street.										
5	A	STOKE		1	W	1-0	1-0	Harris 37	Butler	Rookes	Ferrier	Scoular	Bowler	Dickinson	Harris	Barlow	Reid	Phillips	Froggatt
	4/9		*31,151*	*17*	9				*Herod*	*Mould*	*McCue*	*Mountford F*	*Franklin*	*Sellers*	*Mountford G*	*McAlinden*	*Baker*	*Ormston*	*Steele*
								Ref: W Beckley (Evesham)	Stoke are out of luck as Pompey retain an unbeaten run at all levels (first, reserves and youth). Harris poaches the vital goal, firing home after Herod fails to hold a greasy ball – soaked following a pre-match shower. Baker misses an open goal late on, and sees Rookes head off the line.										
6	H	MIDDLESBROUGH		1	W	1-0	0-0	Reid 87	Butler	Rookes	Ferrier	Scoular	Flewin	Dickinson	Harris	Barlow	Reid	Phillips	Froggatt
	8/9		33,275	*20*	11				*Ugolini*	*Robinson*	*Hepple*	*Gordon*	*Whitaker*	*Blenkinsop*	*Spuhler*	*Dobbie*	*Fenton*	*Dicks*	*Walker*
								Ref: H Williams (London)	Boro battle after a 1-6 loss at Preston, but Reid pinches it, finishing a move started by Dickinson. Just beforehand Spuhler's header grazed a post as ponderous Pompey failed to clear. The attack needs more 'snap' if the team is to be a force concluded 'Ranger' in the *Evening News*.										
7	H	CHARLTON		1	W	3-1	1-0	Reid 41, 52, 75	Butler	Rookes	Ferrier	Scoular	Flewin	Dickinson	Harris	Barlow	Reid	Phillips	Froggatt
	11/9		39,459	*5*	13			*Fenton 61*	*Bartram*	*Campbell*	*Lock*	*Johnson*	*Phipps*	*Whittaker*	*Hurst*	*O'Linn*	*Robinson*	*Fenton*	*Duffy*
								Ref: B Griffiths (Newport, Mon)	Pompey open a three-point gap at the top of the league thanks to Reid's triple. His first came after Phillips' shot deflected into his path, then he headed home Harris' corner. Fenton pulled one back – the first goal conceded since 21 August – but Reid seals it nodding home Phillips' cross.										
8	A	MIDDLESBROUGH		1	D	1-1	0-1	Barlow 53	Butler	Rookes	Ferrier	Scoular	Flewin	Dickinson	Harris	Barlow	Reid	Phillips	Froggatt
	15/9		*33,247*	*13*	14			*Fenton 6*	*Ugolini*	*Robinson*	*Hardwick*	*Gordon*	*Whitaker*	*Blenkinsop*	*Spuhler*	*Dobbie*	*Fenton*	*Dicks*	*Walker*
								Ref: H Williams (London)	Ugolini's blunder costs Boro a point as he fails to deal with Barlow's tame snap-shot as the ball fell to him in the area. Fenton had given Boro the lead when he fired through a crowd of players after the ball came back off the bar. Flewin and Dickinson starred as defences dominated.										
9	A	MANCHESTER C		1	D	1-1	0-1	Reid 65	Butler	Rookes	Ferrier	Scoular	Flewin	Dickinson	Harris	Barlow	Reid	Phillips	Froggatt
	18/9		*51,590*	*12*	15			*McMorran 1*	*Swift*	*Sproston*	*Westwood*	*Fagan*	*McDowell*	*Walsh*	*Oakes*	*Smith*	*McMorran*	*Linacre*	*Clarke*
								Ref: V Rae (London)	A coachload of fans who had travelled overnight welcome the team, but they are stunned by McMorran's opener after Oakes hit the bar. Reid saves it, reacting first when Harris' shot is blocked after Swift misjudges a corner. Late on the post denies him a second and the bar Barlow.										
10	H	SHEFFIELD UTD		1	W	3-0	1-0	Phillips 9, Harris 54, 89	Butler	Rookes	Ferrier	Scoular	Flewin	Dickinson	Harris	Barlow	Reid	Phillips	Froggatt
	25/9		36,240	*20*	17				*Smith*	*Furniss*	*Parkin*	*Jackson*	*Latham*	*Young*	*Jones*	*Thompson*	*Hitchin*	*Ross*	*Collindridge*
								Ref: A Tolley (Worcester)	The South Stand is shut at 1.30 pm on a warm afternoon and the crowd is cheered when Phillips races away to place a cross-shot past Smith. Without displaying their usual fluency, Harris makes it 2-0 driving home after his initial shot hit the keeper, then he wraps it up at the death.										

No	Venue	Opponent	Pos	Res	F-A	H-T	Scorers, Times, and Referees	1	2	3	4	5	6	7	8	9	10	11
11	H	NEWCASTLE	1	W	1-0	0-0	Phillips 65	Butler	Rookes	Ferrier	Scoular	Flewin	Dickinson	Harris	Barlow	Reid	Phillips	Froggatt
2/10		**45,827**	*6*	19				*Fairbrother*	*Cowell*	*Batty*	*Harvey*	*Brennan*	*Dodgin*	*Sibley*	*Stobbart*	*Donaldson*	*Milburn*	*Walker*
							Ref: W Dellow (Croydon)	Newcastle could have drawn level at the top. The gates were closed at 2.[illegible]0, leaving the St John Ambulance to deal with fainting fans. Rookes appears to handle, but the ref refuses Magpies a penalty, then Reid misses from a yard. Phillips holds off a challenge to fire home Reid's pass.										
12	A	ASTON VILLA	1	D	1-1	0-0	Reid 66	Butler	Rookes	Ferrier	Scoular	Flewin	Dickinson	Harris	Barlow	Reid	Phillips	Froggatt
9/10		*57,649*	*20*	20			*Mulraney 72*	*Jones*	*Ashton*	*Cummings*	*Dorsett*	*Parkes*	*Lowe*	*Mulraney*	*Brown*	*Ford*	*Edwards*	*Smith*
							Ref: R Burgess (Reading)	A large Pompey following sees lowly Villa have a let off when Reid heads home, only for the referee to rule Froggatt had crossed from behind the goal-line. Villa crack when Reid wriggles through and rounds the keeper, but Mulraney levels with a fierce shot from the edge of the area.										
13	H	SUNDERLAND	1	W	3-0	2-0	Froggatt 11, Reid 27, Harris 48	Butler	Rookes	Ferrier	Scoular	Flewin	Dickinson	Harris	Barlow	Reid	Phillips	Froggatt
16/10		35,205	*9*	22				*Robinson R*	*Stelling*	*Hudgell*	*Watson*	*Hall*	*Wright*	*Duns*	*Robinson J*	*Shackleton*	*Reynolds*	*Davis*
							Ref: H Pearce (Luton)	Pompey make light of driving rain. Froggatt opens from close in, then Harris crosses for Reid to make it two from 12 yards. The winger makes sure of the win, skipping round Hudgell. Froggatt limped off after a heavy tackle, while Sunderland's Hall lost the toss for the first time in nine.										
14	A	WOLVERHAMPTON	1	L	**0-3**	0-2		Butler	Rookes	Ferrier	Scoular	Flewin	Dickinson	Harris	Barlow	Reid	Phillips	Froggatt
23/10		*48,604*	*13*	22			*Wright 25, Hancocks 28, Smyth 82*	*Williams*	*Kelly*	*Pritchard*	*Crook*	*Shorthouse*	*Wright*	*Hancocks*	*Forbes*	*Pye*	*Smyth*	*Mullen*
							Ref: A Blythe (London)	Monty's congratulatory letter fails to inspire the team, as Wright's 30-yard free-kick sets the tone. Butler lets Hancocks' shot spill from his hands, then an offside denies Reid after the break. Phillips hits the post as the Wolves goal leads a charmed life. Smyth's deflected shot seals it.										
15	H	BOLTON	1	D	0-0	0-0		Butler	Rookes	Ferrier	Scoular	Flewin	Dickinson	Harris	Phillips	Reid	Barlow	Froggatt
30/10		29,760	*14*	23				*Elvy*	*Hamlett*	*Banks*	*Howe*	*Barrass*	*Murphy*	*Woodward*	*Hernon*	*Moir*	*Bradley*	*McShane*
							Ref: H Hauxwell (W Wickham)	Derby win to take over at the top, as lacklustre Pompey fail to break down Bolton. Elvy is their hero, making a string of fine interceptions and Trotters might have won with better finishing. Boss Jackson's Scottish scouting trip needs to bear fruit and freshen up the side says 'Ranger'.										
16	A	LIVERPOOL	2	L	1-3	1-2	Harris 33	Butler	Rookes	Ferrier	Scoular	Flewin	Dickinson	Harris	Phillips	Reid	Barlow	Froggatt
6/11		*43,665*	*11*	23			*Liddell 8, Balmer 18, Done 77*	*Sidlow*	*Shepherd*	*Lambert*	*Taylor*	*Jones*	*Fagan*	*Payne*	*Balmer*	*Done*	*Liddell*	*Brierley*
							Ref: H Hartley (Chelmsford)	One future Pool boss – Fagan – comes in for another, the injured Paisley. Liddell's 18-yard header opens, then he sets up Balmer with a lovely flick for a simple finish. Harris nets with an angled shot and Barlow rattles the bar as Pompey rally. Done settles it after good work by Payne.										
17	H	BLACKPOOL	2	D	1-1	0-0	Harris 84	Butler	Rookes	Ferrier	Scoular	Flewin	Dickinson	Harris	**Delapenha**	Reid	Clarke	Froggatt
13/11		44,869	*13*	24			*Mortensen 82p*	*Farm*	*Shimwell*	*Suart*	*Johnston*	*Hayward*	*Kelly*	*Matthews*	*Rickett*	*McIntosh*	*Mortensen*	*Wardle*
							Ref: F Green (Wolverhampton)	Jamaican Delapenha is Pompey's first black player and Clarke replaces Phillips, but still the attack fires blanks. The ref courts controversy as Rookes supposedly fouls McIntosh and Mortensen converts. Harris levels almost at once and news of Derby's loss brightens the mood further.										
18	A	DERBY	3	L	0-1	0-0		Butler	Rookes	Ferrier	Scoular	Flewin	Dickinson	Harris	Delapenha	Clarke	Barlow	Froggatt
20/11		*34,042*	*1*	24			*Steel 46*	*Townsend*	*Mozley*	*Howe*	*Ward*	*Leuty*	*Musson*	*Harrison*	*Powell*	*Stamps*	*Steel*	*Broome*
							Ref: G Clark (London)	Rams go four points clear with this win. Stamps hit a post in a thrilling first half and Pompey crack when Steel's cross-shot beats Butler after Flewin lost the ball in the sun. Harris's mazy dribbles and pin-point crosses are scorned, to the anguish of an estimated 1,200 travelling fans.										
19	H	ARSENAL	3	W	4-1	2-0	Froggatt 9, Clarke 12, Phillips 54, [Barlow 89]	Butler	Rookes	Ferrier	Scoular	Flewin	Dickinson	Harris	Barlow	Clarke	Phillips	Froggatt
27/11		42,500	*5*	26			*Lewis 70p*	*Swindin*	*Banes*	*Smith*	*Macauley*	*Compton*	*Mercer*	*Roper*	*Logie*	*Lewis*	*Forbes*	*McPherson*
							Ref: B Griffiths (Newport, Mon)	A 'Go(a)lden Jubilee' crowed the *Football Mail*. With Monty watching, Arsenal have yet to let in two in a game, but Froggatt's snap-shot and Clarke's turn and shot change that. A poor back-pass sees Phillips profit, then Barlow nets Clarke's cross after Scoular fouled Roper in the box.										
20	A	HUDDERSFIELD	2	D	0-0	0-0		Butler	Rookes	Ferrier	Scoular	Flewin	Dickinson	Harris	Barlow	Clarke	Phillips	Froggatt
4/12		*21,785*	*19*	27				*Mills*	*Hayes*	*Briggs*	*Whittaker*	*Hepplewhite*	*Boot*	*Smith*	*Nightingale*	*Doherty*	*McKenna*	*Glazzard*
							Ref: G Iliffe (Leicester)	Pompey, playing in red, squander a point and might even have lost to their lowly hosts. Derby's five-goal win over Charlton means they re-open a three-point lead. Doherty's lob drifted just over on half-time, then Glazzard missed from four yards. Phillips almost pinched it late on.										
21	H	MANCHESTER U	3	D	2-2	0-1	Froggatt 60, Clarke 63	Butler	Rookes	Ferrier	Scoular	Flewin	Dickinson	Harris	Barlow	Clarke	Phillips	Froggatt
11/12		29,966	*4*	28			*Mitten 44p, McGlen 87*	*Crompton*	*Carey*	*Aston*	*Cockburn*	*Chilton*	*McGlen*	*Delaney*	*Morris*	*Rowley*	*Pearson*	*Mitten*
							Ref: H Pearce (Luton)	Mitten gives United the lead when Flewin upends him, but Froggatt's 20-yarder and Clarke's finish after good work by Barlow seem to have turned the game. Butler is left groggy by Rowley's piledriver and in the dying minutes McGlen nods home as United force a string of corners.										

LEAGUE DIVISION 1 — Manager: Bob Jackson — SEASON 1948-49

No		Date	Att	Pos	Pt	F-A	H-T	Scorers, Times, and Referees	1	2	3	4	5	6	7	8	9	10	11
22	H	PRESTON		2	W	3-1	2-0	Harris 10, Phillips 33, Barlow 49p	Butler	Rookes	Ferrier	Scoular	Flewin	Dickinson	Harris	Barlow	Clarke	Phillips	Froggatt
		18/12	**26,545**	*20*	30			*Brown 87*	*Newlands*	*Walton*	*Kane*	*Davie*	*Waters*	*Dougall*	*Brown*	*Knight*	*McIntosh*	*Jackson*	*Langton*
								Ref: L Brown (Barnes)	Proud Preston are anything but as Pompey stroll home. Barlow and Clarke combine to set up Harris, then Froggatt slips a pass to Phillips who makes no mistake. Waters chops down Harris, but Barlow has the luck as Newlands blocks the penalty only for the ball to creep over the line.										
23	A	CHELSEA		1	W	2-1	0-1	Harris 57, 65	Butler	Rookes	Ferrier	Scoular	Flewin	Dickinson	Harris	Barlow	Clarke	Phillips	Froggatt
		25/12	*42,153*	*16*	32			*Jones 20*	*Pickering*	*Bathgate*	*Hughes*	*Armstrong*	*Harris*	*Macauley*	*Jones*	*Bowie*	*Bentley*	*Walker*	*McInnes*
								Ref: C Wakely (Somerton)	Pompey are the only one in the top five to win and return to the top of the table. However, Chelsea, with Walker playing his last game, have the better of the first half. Jones' rising drive trumps Butler, but once Harris levels Pompey take charge. Harris nets Barlow's centre to seal it.										
24	H	CHELSEA		1	W	5-2	3-1	Harris 2, 23, Clarke 37, Winter 77 (og), [Barlow 79p]	Butler	Rookes	Ferrier	Scoular	Flewin	Dickinson	Harris	Barlow	Clarke	Phillips	Froggatt
		26/12	43,624	*16*	34			*Bentley 15, 70*	*Pickering*	*Bathgate*	*Winter*	*Armstrong*	*Harris*	*Macauley*	*Campbell*	*Bowie*	*Bentley*	*Jones*	*Walker*
								Ref: C Wakley (Somerton)	Pompey go 'nap' but the result is always in the balance until Winter hooks into his own net under pressure from Clarke. Harris' cross-shot is the perfect start, but Bentley's persistence keeps Chelsea in it, his second from a narrow angle. Barlow netted from the spot after Harris was fouled.										
25	A	BURNLEY		1	L	1-2	1-1	Bray 19 (og)	Butler	Rookes	Ferrier	Scoular	Flewin	Dickinson	Harris	Barlow	Clarke	Phillips	Froggatt
		1/1	*31,045*	*15*	34			*Chew 12, McLaren 70*	*Strong*	*Loughran*	*Mather*	*Attwell*	*Woodruff*	*Bray*	*Chew*	*McLaren*	*Billingham*	*Potts*	*Hays*
								Ref: J Tregallas (Birmingham)	Turf Moor remains a 'bogey': Pompey have still to get a point there. Chew gobbles up the opener when Butler fails to clear a cross, but poor Bray levels as his back-pass strands the keeper. Snow and poor light close in as Burnley take their prize scalp when McLaren is set up by Potts.										
26	H	STOKE		1	W	1-0	0-0	Froggatt 57	Butler	Yeuell	Ferrier	Scoular	Flewin	Dickinson	Harris	Barlow	Clarke	Phillips	Froggatt
		15/1	34,538	*7*	36				*Herod*	*Meakin*	*McCue*	*Mountford F*	*Franklin*	*Sellars*	*Mountford G*	*Bowyer*	*Peppitt*	*Ormston*	*Steele*
								Ref: W Beckley (Worcester)	A frustrating first half ends with Pompey denied a penalty when two Stoke players appear to handle. Froggatt is then upset when the referee gives a free-kick as he gets away from a foul, but he is soon celebrating as his place kick deceives the keeper who can only help it over the line.										
27	A	CHARLTON		1	W	1-0	1-0	Clarke 23	Butler	Yeuell	Ferrier	Scoular	Flewin	Dickinson	Harris	Barlow	Clarke	Phillips	Froggatt
		22/1	***61,475***	*5*	38				*Bartram*	*Campbell*	*Lock*	*Fenton*	*Phipps*	*Revell*	*Hurst*	*O'Linn*	*Vaughan*	*Purves*	*Duffy*
								Ref: B Griffiths (Newport, Mon)	Clarke delights a travelling army of fans with a low shot which Bartram couldn't hold. The win opens a three-point gap at the top of the table as Magpies are held at Stoke. Back at Fratton, Reid steps up his claim for a recall with five goals in the 6-0 reserve drubbing of West Ham.										
28	H	MANCHESTER C		1	W	3-1	0-1	Clarke 70, 88, Harris 77	Butler	Yeuell	Ferrier	Scoular	Flewin	Dickinson	Harris	Barlow	Clarke	Phillips	Froggatt
		5/2	34,949	*9*	40			*Smith 3*	*Swift*	*Sproston*	*Westwood*	*Walsh*	*Fagan*	*Emptage*	*Oakes*	*Hart*	*Smith*	*Linacre*	*Clark*
								Ref: V Rae (London)	Monty's pre-match telegram from Switzerland urges the team to concentrate on the league. With the help of the 'Chimes' they do just that after Smith nods City in front. After Clarke's overhead kick, it's one-way traffic. Harris poaches the lead, then Clarke scores with a first-time shot.										
29	A	SHEFFIELD UTD		1	L	1-3	1-1	Barlow 2	Butler	Yeuell	Ferrier	Scoular	Flewin	Dickinson	Froggatt	Barlow	Clarke	Phillips	Parker
		19/2	*42,876*	*18*	40			*Hitchen 12, Hagan 48, Collindridge 75*	*White*	*Bailey*	*Cox*	*Hitchen*	*Latham*	*Shaw*	*Jones*	*Hagan*	*Smith*	*Brook*	*Collindridge*
								Ref: A Colley (Worcester)	Pompey fail to impress the watching FA international selection committee chairman. Barlow scores from close in, only for Hitchen to level from 20 yards. Injured Flewin isn't there for the re-start, but when he returns, Hagan has already flashed home. Collindridge makes it safe.										
30	H	ASTON VILLA		1	W	3-0	1-0	Phillips 35, 63, Froggatt 87	Butler	Yeuell	Ferrier	Scoular	Flewin	Dickinson	Harris	Barlow	Clarke	Phillips	Froggatt
		5/3	34,264	*18*	42				*Rutherford*	*Parkes*	*Cummings*	*Powell*	*Martin*	*Moss*	*Gibson*	*Dixon*	*Ford*	*Dorsett*	*Smith*
								Ref: R Burgess (Reading)	Villa's recent run of form comes to an abrupt halt. Phillips nods home at the second attempt, then he makes the points safe with a 30-yard shot on the spin. Froggatt's diving header rounds things off, while boss Jackson was elsewhere, with two directors, watching a potential signing.										
31	A	SUNDERLAND		1	W	4-1	3-1	Froggatt 25, Reid 31, 51, Phillips 35	Butler	Yeuell	Ferrier	Scoular	Flewin	Dickinson	Harris	Reid	Froggatt	Phillips	Parker
		12/3	*57,229*	*15*	44			*Broadis 10*	*Mapson*	*Stelling*	*Hudgell*	*Watson*	*Oliver*	*Wright A*	*Wright T*	*Broadis*	*Shackleton*	*Reynolds*	*Turnbull*
								Ref: H Pearce (Luton)	A coachload from Rosyth dockyard see their team go five points clear at the top. Broadis fired home, but Froggatt's header and the returning Reid's left footer turned the game. Mapson's flap at Harris' cross left Phillips with an easy job, before Reid fired home through a crowded box.										

No	Venue	Opponent / Att	Pos	Res / Pts	FT	HT	Scorers / Referee	1	2	3	4	5	6	7	8	9	10	11
32	H	DERBY	1	W	1-0	1-0	Phillips 17	Butler	Yeuell	Ferrier	Scoular	Flewin	Dickinson	Harris	Reid	Froggatt	Phillips	Parker
19/3		43,188	*3*	46				*Webster*	*Parr*	*Howe*	*Mozley*	*Leuty*	*Musson*	*Harrison*	*Morris*	*Thompson*	*Stamps*	*Broome*
							Ref: G Clark (London)	Defending the 'station' end – KJC or Fratton in new money – in the first half, Portsmouth are in control throughout against a chief title rival. Froggatt's pass unleashes Phillips whose left-foot drive settles it, and but for two fine saves from Webster late on he might have had a hat-trick.										
33	H	LIVERPOOL	1	W	3-2	2-0	Clarke 22, Harris 25, Phillips 48	Butler	Hindmarsh	Ferrier	Scoular	Flewin	Dickinson	Harris	Reid	Clarke	Phillips	Froggatt
2/4		35,013	*11*	48			*Stubbins 54, Paisley 57*	*Sidlow*	*Shepherd*	*Lambert*	*Williams*	*Hughes*	*Paisley*	*Payne*	*Balmer*	*Stubbins*	*Done*	*Liddell*
							Ref: H Hartley (Chelmsford)	Pompey have 20 top-flight wins for the first time. Clarke glances home from a corner to open, then Harris's pace allows him to get clear and steer home. Phillips' drive seems to have sealed it, but Stubbins and Paisley take advantage of some slack defending to set up a tense finale.										
34	A	NEWCASTLE	1	W	**5-0**	3-0	Froggatt 6, 34, 87, Harris 37, 82	Butler	Hindmarsh	Ferrier	Scoular	Flewin	Dickinson	Harris	Reid	Clarke	Phillips	Froggatt
6/4		*60,611*	*2*	50				*Fairbrother*	*Cowell*	*Batty*	*Harvey*	*Brennan*	*Dodgin*	*Walker*	*Robledo*	*Stobbart*	*Taylor*	*Mitchell*
							Ref: W Dellow (Croydon)	Pompey tighten their title grip with five headed goals, making their nearest rivals look ordinary. The pick is Froggatt's diving effort to make it 2-0, settling the team after a tricky spell. Only Scoular – 'still prone to keep the ball too close' according to 'Ranger' – comes in for any criticism.										
35	A	BLACKPOOL	1	L	0-1	0-0		Butler	Hindmarsh	Ferrier	Scoular	Flewin	Dickinson	Harris	Reid	Clarke	Phillips	Froggatt
9/4		***18,723***	*11*	50			*Adams 53*	*Farm*	*Shimwell*	*Suart*	*Fenton*	*Hayward*	*Kelly*	*Adams*	*McCall*	*McIntosh*	*Davidson*	*Wardle*
							Ref: F Green (Wolverhampton)	Adams is offside, claim Pompey, as he runs on to a through-ball and fires past Butler, but there is no doubt Pool deserve the points. As tension mounts Scoular is booked for a foul near the end, and news of Newcastle's win (4-2 at Derby) means any title celebrations are still on ice.										
36	H	BIRMINGHAM	1	W	3-1	0-1	Reid 52, 55, Clarke 70	Butler	Hindmarsh	Ferrier	Scoular	Flewin	Dickinson	Harris	Reid	Clarke	Phillips	Froggatt
15/4		38,456	*13*	52			*Dorman 41*	*Merrick*	*Green*	*Jennings*	*Badham*	*Duckhouse*	*Ferris*	*Stewart*	*Jordan*	*Dailly*	*Dorman*	*Laing*
							Ref: W Edwards (Yeovil)	A powerful second half calms nerves after lowly City had pinched the lead with only their 32nd goal in 37 matches. Reid's header and a typical piledriver turn the game as he atones for an earlier missed sitter. Phillips and Clarke both rattle the bar, before Clarke's stinging shot settles it.										
37	H	WOLVERHAMPTON	1	W	**5-0**	3-0	Phillips 6, Reid 44, 48, Clarke 7, 70	Butler	Hindmarsh	Ferrier	Scoular	Flewin	Dickinson	Harris	Reid	Clarke	Phillips	Froggatt
16/4		44,225	*8*	54				*Williams*	*Springthorpe*	*Pritchard*	*Crooks*	*Chatham*	*Baxter*	*Hancocks*	*Forbes*	*Wilshaw*	*Dunn*	*Smith*
							Ref: A Blythe (London)	Shirt-sleeved fans see Phillips fire home and quick-thinking Clarke nip in to score. Butler is redundant in a first half which ends with Reid crashing home Ferrier's pass. Another thunderbolt makes it four, then Harris and Scoular set up Clarke to net Pompey's 50th at Fratton so far.										
38	A	BIRMINGHAM	1	L	0-3	0-1	*[Hindmarsh 80 (og)]*	Butler	Hindmarsh	Ferrier	Scoular	Flewin	Dickinson	Harris	Reid	Clarke	Phillips	Parker
18/4		*29,983*	*11*	54			*Stewart 32, Badham 68,*	*Merrick*	*Mardonal*	*Green*	*Dornan*	*Duckhouse*	*Ferris*	*Berry*	*Jordan*	*Badham*	*Stewart*	*Laing*
							Ref: W Edwards (Yeovil)	Dickinson's cut head on half-time means he has to swap with Phillips and Pompey never look like getting back into it. City score three for the first time since December, Hindmarsh's back-pass completing the rout. Newcastle go down 2-3 at Boro, meaning two more points should do.										
39	A	BOLTON	1	W	2-1	2-0	Harris 3, Clarke 25	Butler	Hindmarsh	Ferrier	Scoular	Flewin	Dickinson	Harris	Reid	Clarke	Phillips	Froggatt
23/4		*28,816*	*17*	56			*Roberts 82*	*Elvy*	*Roberts*	*Banks*	*Howe*	*Barrass*	*Murphy*	*Moir*	*Dillon*	*Lofthouse*	*Bradley*	*McShane*
							Ref: H Hoxley (Kent)	Pompey are Champions after their rivals drop points, but Roberts' late goal makes Pompey fight for the crucial victory after Clarke and Harris had set each other up early on. The team is celebrating tonight with a meal in London, before a coach ride back to the city early tomorrow.										
40	H	HUDDERSFIELD	1	W	2-0	1-0	Reid 19p, Clarke 83	Butler	Hindmarsh	Ferrier	Scoular	Flewin	Thompson	Harris	Reid	Clarke	Phillips	Froggatt
30/4		37,042	*22*	58				*Mills*	*Stewart*	*Hayes*	*Boot*	*Hepplewhite*	*Whittaker*	*Metcalfe*	*Nightingale*	*Glazzard*	*Hansen*	*McKenna*
							Ref: H Williams (Fulham)	Flewin receives the trophy from EJ Cearns of the Football League, as fans flood the pitch. Monty – of course – is there, but Dickinson's head injury means he misses his first ever game due to injury. Hepplewhite's handball allowed Reid to convert, then he set up Clarke to fire home.										
41	A	ARSENAL	1	L	2-3	1-2	Clarke 15, 82	Butler	Hindmarsh	Thompson	Scoular	Flewin	Dickinson	Parker	Reid	Clarke	Phillips	Froggatt
4/5		*56,973*	*5*	58			*Lishman 9, 35, Logie 80*	*Swindin*	*Barnes*	*Smith L*	*Macauley*	*Compton L*	*Forbes*	*McPherson*	*Logie*	*Roper*	*Lishman*	*Vallance*
							Ref: B Griffiths (Newport, Mon)	Arsenal heavily water the pitch to slow down Pompey. Early on recalled Parker's header hit the post, then at the death Clarke's effort is ruled out for handball. In between, Lishman and Logie had profited from some slack defending. Harris is off playing for Football League in Belfast.										
42	A	MANCHESTER U	1	L	2-3	2-2	Reid 25, Harris 35	Butler	Hindmarsh	Yeuell	Scoular	Thompson	Dickinson	Harris	Reid	Clarke	Phillips	Froggatt
7/5		*52,661*	*2*	58			*Rowley 12, 54, Mitten 42p*	*Crompton*	*Carey*	*Aston*	*Anderson*	*Chilton*	*Cockburn*	*Delaney*	*Downie*	*Rowley*	*Pearson*	*Mitten*
Average	Home 37,058	Away 42,041					Ref: H Pearce (Luton)	Ten-man Pompey – Harris hobbled off in the second half – should have had a point, but Reid sees his late penalty saved after a handball. An all-action first half saw Reid's back-heel and Harris' header cancel out Rowley's drive, but Mitten levels from the spot after Yeuell fouled him.										

LEAGUE DIVISION 1 (CUP-TIES) **Manager: Bob Jackson** **SEASON 1948-49**

FA Cup					F-A	H-T	Scorers, Times, and Referees	1	2	3	4	5	6	7	8	9	10	11
3	H	STOCKPORT	1	W	7-0	3-0	Phillips 21, 67, Harris 22 ,82, 88,	Butler	Rookes	Ferrier	Scoular	Flewin	Dickinson	Harris	Barlow	Clarke	Phillips	Froggatt
8/1		33,590 *3N:9*					[Clarke 41, 65]	*Bowles*	*Staniforth*	*Monks*	*McCulloch*	*Easdale*	*Paterson*	*Dainty*	*Walker*	*Swinscoe*	*Herd*	*Brown*
							Ref: S Beasley (Burbage)	Barlow sends Phillips clear, then Harris is given time and space as Pompey show their class. Clarke scores from point blank, then two quick goals let the limping Rookes leave the field. Harris nabbed a hat-trick late on, bracketing County's best effort which was cleared off the line.										
4	H	SHEFFIELD WED	1	W	2-1	1-1	Harris 23, Phillips 60	Butler	Yeuell	Ferrier	Scoular	Flewin	Dickinson	Harris	Barlow	Clarke	Phillips	Froggatt
29/1		47,188 *2:6*					*Quigley 20*	*McIntosh*	*Westlake*	*Swift*	*Locherty*	*Turton*	*Witcomb*	*Kilshaw*	*Quigley*	*Froggatt*	*Woodhead*	*Jordan*
							Ref: H Hartley (Chelmsford)	Yeovil stun Sunderland today, but Pompey avoid a cup shock of their own against Owls despite trailing to Quigley's close-range effort. Harris nods home a corner almost at once, then Phillips is put clear to round the keeper. Both teams were in a change strip because of the colour clash.										
5	H	NEWPORT	1	W	3-2	1-2	Phillips 5, 55, Froggatt 115	Butler	Yeuell	Ferrier	Scoular	Flewin	Dickinson	Harris	Barlow	Clarke	Phillips	Froggatt
12/2		48,581 *3S:20*			*aet*		*Harper 15, Carr 31*	*Grant*	*Bradford*	*Hayward*	*Roffi*	*Wilcox*	*Newall*	*Williams*	*Comley*	*Parker*	*Carr*	*Harper*
							Ref: E Vickery (Bristol)	County beat Terriers in round four, but a record crowd sits back after Phillips' tap in. Harper, then Carr from close range, stand the game on its head, but Phillips levels. In extra-time Comley misses a sitter, Barlow has a penalty saved after a handball. Froggatt spares Pompey blushes.										
QF	H	DERBY	1	W	2-1	1-1	Clarke 44, 87	Butler	Yeuell	Ferrier	Scoular	Flewin	Dickinson	Harris	Barlow	Clarke	Phillips	Froggatt
26/2		51,385 *3*					*Stamps 41*	*Townsend*	*Parr*	*Howe*	*Mozley*	*Leuty*	*Musson*	*Harrison*	*Powell*	*Stamps*	*Steel*	*Broome*
							Ref: W Ling (Cambridge)	Clarke's left foot puts Pompey in the semis, moments after Broome had seen Butler smother his close-range shot. The gates shut at 2 pm on a record-breaking crowd, paying £5,465 17s to see Stamps head home Harrison's corner only for Clarke to reply in kind from Froggatt's centre.										
SF	N	LEICESTER	1	L	1-3	1-1	Harris 25	Butler	Yeuell	Ferrier	Scoular	Flewin	Dickinson	Harris	Barlow	Clarke	Phillips	Froggatt
26/3		62,000 *2:20*					*Revie 5, 55, Chisholm 47*	*McGraw*	*Jelly*	*Scott*	*Harrison*	*Plummer*	*King*	*Griffiths*	*Revie*	*Lee*	*Chisholm*	*Adam*
		(at Highbury)					Ref: H Pearce (Luton)	Harris's miss from six yards, just after Chisholm had regained City's lead, turns this tie. Lowly Leicester, inspired by Revie, went ahead with his cool finish. Harris steadied the ship, holding off a strong challenge to net, but Pompey fold once Butler lets Revie's header squirm home.										

		Home					Away					
	P	W	D	L	F	A	W	D	L	F	A	Pts
1 PORTSMOUTH	42	18	3	0	52	12	7	5	9	32	30	58
2 Manchester U	42	11	7	3	40	20	10	4	7	37	24	53
3 Derby	42	17	2	2	48	22	5	7	9	26	33	53
4 Newcastle	42	12	5	4	35	29	8	7	6	35	27	52
5 Arsenal	42	13	5	3	51	18	5	8	8	23	26	49
6 Wolves	42	13	5	3	48	19	4	7	10	31	47	46
7 Manchester C	42	10	8	3	28	21	5	7	9	19	30	45
8 Sunderland	42	8	10	3	27	19	5	7	9	22	39	43
9 Charlton	42	10	5	6	38	31	5	7	9	25	36	42
10 Aston Villa	42	10	6	5	40	36	6	4	11	20	40	42
11 Stoke	42	14	3	4	43	24	2	6	13	23	44	41
12 Liverpool	42	5	10	6	25	18	8	4	9	28	25	40
13 Chelsea	42	10	6	5	43	27	2	8	11	26	41	38
14 Bolton	42	10	4	7	43	32	4	6	11	16	36	38
15 Burnley	42	10	6	5	27	19	2	8	11	16	31	38
16 Blackpool	42	8	8	5	24	25	3	8	10	30	42	38
17 Birmingham	42	9	7	5	19	10	2	8	11	17	28	37
18 Everton	42	12	5	4	33	25	1	6	14	8	38	37
19 Middlesbro	42	10	6	5	37	23	1	6	14	9	34	34
20 Huddersfield	42	6	7	8	19	24	6	3	12	21	45	34
21 Preston	42	8	6	7	36	36	3	5	13	26	39	33
22 Sheffield Utd	42	8	9	4	32	25	3	2	16	25	53	33
	924	232	133	97	788	515	97	133	232	515	788	924

Odds & ends

Double wins: (6) Everton, Stoke, Newcastle, Chelsea, Sunderland, Charlton.
Double losses: (0).

Won from behind: (4) Chelsea (a), Manchester C (h), Sunderland (a), Birmingham (h).
Lost from in front: (2) Sheffield Utd (a), Manchester U (a).

High spots: Winning 5-0 at title rivals Newcastle in April.
Going unbeaten in all 21 league and four FA Cup-ties at Fratton.
Beating Arsenal 4-1 at home in the Golden Jubilee match in November.

Low spot: Losing 1-3 to second division Leicester in the FA Cup semi-final at Highbury.

97 of Pompey's 99 league and FA Cup goals were shared between just six players – all forwards. The other two were own-goals.

Hat-tricks: (2) Reid and Froggatt.
Ever-presents: (2) Butler and Scoular.
Leading Scorer: Reid and Harris (17).

	Appearances		Goals		
	Lge	FAC	Lge	FAC	Tot
Barlow, Bert	29	*5*	9		9
Bowler, Gerry	2				
Butler, Ernie	42	5			
Clarke, Ike	24	*5*	14	4	18
Delapenha, Lindy	2				
Dickinson, Jim	41	*5*			
Ferrier, Harry	40	*5*			
Flewin, Reg	39	*5*			
Froggatt, Jack	41	*5*	14	1	15
Harris, Peter	40	*5*	17	5	22
Hindmarsh, Billy	10				
Parker, Cliff	5				
Phillips, Len	40	*5*	11	5	16
Reid, Duggie	29		17		17
Rookes, Phil	25	*1*			
Scoular, Jimmy	42	*5*			
Thompson, Bill	3				
Yeuell, Jasper	8	*4*			
(own-goals)			2		2
18 players used	**462**	**55**	**84**	**15**	**99**

LEAGUE DIVISION 1 | Manager: Bob Jackson | SEASON 1949-50

No	Date		Att	Pos	Pt	F-A	H-T	Scorers, Times, and Referees	1	2	3	4	5	6	7	8	9	10	11
1	A	NEWCASTLE			W	3-1	2-0	Phillips 9, Clarke 41, Harris 52	Butler	Yeuell	Ferrier	Scoular	Flewin	Dickinson	Harris	Reid	Clarke	Phillips	Froggatt
	20/8		*54,258*		2			*Robledo 68*	*Fairbrother*	*Craig*	*Batty*	*Houghton*	*Brennan*	*Dodgin*	*Walker*	*Robledo*	*Milburn*	*Lowrie*	*Mitchell*
								Ref: H Williams (Fulham)	Pompey show their title was no fluke as Geordies are outclassed. Phillips and Clarke finish coolly, sandwiching a spicy clash between Chilean Robledo and Phillips. Harris' close-range goal seems to have settled it, but Robledo's opportunism from Milburn's shot makes a lively finish.										
2	H	MANCHESTER C		5	D	1-1	1-1	Reid 36p	Butler	Yeuell	Ferrier	Scoular	Flewin	Dickinson	Harris	Reid	Clarke	Phillips	Froggatt
	24/8		43,965	*10*	3			*Munro 37*	*Powell*	*Williams*	*Westwood*	*Walsh*	*Fagan*	*Emptage*	*Linacre*	*Munro*	*Smith*	*Black*	*Clarke*
								Ref: W Muller (London)	This game should have been won by half-time, but Pompey miss three chances and only had Reid's penalty when, Walsh handled a cross, to show. Within moments Munro netted after a scramble. Late on Pompey might have had a second pen. Powell (19) made City debut in goal.										
3	H	BLACKPOOL		9	L	2-3	1-1	Clarke 12, Phillips 51	Butler	Yeuell	Ferrier	Scoular	Flewin	Dickinson	Harris	Reid	Clarke	Phillips	Froggatt
	27/8		47,260	*4*	3			*McIntosh 42, Mortensen 57, 86*	*Farm*	*Garnett*	*Suart*	*Johnston*	*Hayward*	*Kelly*	*Matthews*	*Mortensen*	*McIntosh*	*McCall*	*Rickett*
								Ref: L Thompson (Worksop)	The last home defeat was Boxing Bay 1947. Clarke bulldozes home after Farm's save, then McIntosh heads level. Phillips nods home a corner, but poor defending lets the persistent Mortensen in twice. Matthews was at the Fratton Road Co-op this morning promoting his brand of boots.										
4	A	MANCHESTER C		15	L	0-1	0-0		Butler	Hindmarsh	Ferrier	Scoular	Flewin	Dickinson	Harris	Reid	Clarke	Phillips	Froggatt
	31/8		*32,631*	*14*	3			*Smith 49*	*Swift*	*Williams*	*Westwood*	*Walsh*	*Fagan*	*Emptage*	*Linacre*	*Munro*	*Smith*	*Black*	*Clarke*
								Ref: W Muller (London)	'What's wrong with your team?' asks a *Daily Express* reporter. 'I don't know. You tell me,' replies Jackson. Pompey have all the possession, but ordinary City nick it when Munro's run and shot falls kindly for Smith. A fan runs on to threaten the ref when he ignores a City penalty appeal.										
5	A	MIDDLESBROUGH		8	W	5-1	2-1	Fr'ggatt 17, Cl'rke 32, H'rris 75, 86, 88	Butler	Hindmarsh	Ferrier	Scoular	Flewin	Dickinson	Harris	Delapenha	Clarke	Phillips	Froggatt
	3/9		*41,974*	*18*	5			*McKennan 18p*	*Ugolini*	*Robinson*	*Hepple*	*Bell*	*Rickaby*	*Dicks*	*Spuhler*	*McKennan*	*McCrae*	*Mannion*	*Walker*
								Ref: W Ling (Cambridge)	There was a healthy gate despite a bus strike and the result is just the ticket. Froggatt heads home, but Boro bounce back when referee and line agree McCrae was fouled. Clarke restored the lead from close, then Froggatt hit the bar. Harris shows his versatility with two shots and header.										
6	A	ASTON VILLA		12	L	0-1	0-0		Butler	Hindmarsh	Ferrier	Scoular	Flewin	Dickinson	Harris	Delapenha	Clarke	Phillips	Froggatt
	5/9		*38,360*	*9*	5			*Powell 55*	*Rutherford*	*Parkes*	*Dorsett*	*Powell*	*Martin*	*Moss*	*Gibson*	*Dixon*	*Craddock*	*Harrison*	*Goffin*
								Ref: A Blythe (London)	Ten-man Pompey – Delapenha comes off injured at half-time – are still firing blanks, but they deserve a draw here, after a late rally. Wales international and Villa captain Powell heads home a Goffin free-kick. Villa defended superbly and Pompey took 80 minutes to force a corner.										
7	H	EVERTON		9	W	**7-0**	2-0	Froggatt 4, Reid 39, 49, 85, Phillips 63, [Harris 72, Clarke 78]	Butler	Hindmarsh	Ferrier	Scoular	Flewin	Dickinson	Harris	Reid	Clarke	Phillips	Froggatt
	10/9		36,094	*8*					*Sagar*	*Saunders*	*Dugdale*	*Farrell*	*Jones*	*Lello*	*Corr*	*Wainwright*	*Catterick*	*Fielding*	*Eglington*
								Ref: W Rogers (Birmingham)	Reid's returns with a triple as Toffees come unstuck. Froggatt starts it with a fierce shot, then Reid's pile-driver free-kick leaves Sagar helpless. Everton deserve more, but Pompey are majestic. It's the best league win since 1924 and the last three against Everton have a 16-0 aggregate!										
8	A	HUDDERSFIELD		7	W	1-0	0-0	Clarke 60	Butler	Hindmarsh	Ferrier	Scoular	Flewin	Dickinson	Harris	Reid	Clarke	Phillips	Froggatt
	17/9		*26,222*	*20*	9				*Hesford*	*Howe*	*Stewart*	*Hunter*	*Percival*	*Boot*	*McKenna*	*Glazzard*	*Rodgers*	*Nightingale*	*Metcalfe*
								Ref: H Pearce (London)	Red-shirted Pompey are too good for Town (who had nine men out injured) without ever playing as well as last week. Clarke secures the vital goal, turning home from close range after Harris had skinned Stewart. Pompey should have netted more, but late casualness nearly let Town in.										
9	H	BOLTON		7	D	1-1	1-1	Clarke 19	Butler	Yeuell	Ferrier	Scoular	Flewin	Dickinson	Harris	Reid	Clarke	Phillips	Froggatt
	24/9		35,765	*13*	10			*Lofthouse 26*	*Hanson*	*Roberts*	*Kinsell*	*Howe*	*Gillies*	*Murphy*	*Woodward*	*Hernon*	*Lofthouse*	*Bradley*	*McShane*
								Ref: E Vickery (Bristol)	The team is snapped beforehand with Monty and the title, but this is a let down. It looks good when Harris and Reid combine for Clarke to stab in, but Yeuell is caught out and Lofthouse nets. In the second half Phillips hit the bar, but Wolves are setting the pace with seven wins in eight.										
10	H	WOLVERHAMPTON		7	D	1-1	1-0	Reid 30p	Butler	Hindmarsh	Ferrier	Scoular	Thompson	Dickinson	Harris	Reid	Clarke	Phillips	Froggatt
	1/10		**50,248**	*1*	11			*Pye 57*	*Williams*	*Kelly*	*Springthorpe*	*Crook*	*Shorthouse*	*Wright*	*Hancocks*	*Forbes*	*Pye*	*Wilshaw*	*Mullen*
								Ref: G Clark (London)	Before a record league gate, Pompey fail to dent Wolves' commanding lead. With seven internationals between them, this is top quality stuff. Pompey led when Springthorpe handled and Reid converted the pen, but then Ferrier and Hindmarsh got in a tangle and Pye pounced to level.										

No	H/A	Opponent / Date	Att	Pos	Res	Pts	F-A	H-T	Scorers, Times, Referees	1	2	3	4	5	6	7	8	9	10	11
11	A	BIRMINGHAM		6	W		3-0	3-0	Clarke 21, 33, Reid 34	Butler	Hindmarsh	Ferrier	Scoular	Thompson	Dickinson	Harris	Reid	Clarke	Phillips	Froggatt
		8/10	*37,944*	*22*		13				*Merrick*	*Trigg*	*Green*	*Harris*	*McDonnell*	*Badham*	*Berry*	*Brennan*	*Dailly*	*Capel*	*Ferris*
									Ref: W Edwards (Yeovil)	Fresh from a friendly win at Clyde, Pompey are delayed by train troubles, but make up lost time with an express start. Ike Clarke nods home a corner, then his shot creeps under Merrick. Harris claims a hat-trick of assists, before Green limps off (torn thigh). Berry heads against the bar.										
12	H	DERBY		4	W		3-1	2-0	Reid 8, Clarke 32, Froggatt 65	Butler	Hindmarsh	Ferrier	Scoular	Thompson	**Pickett**	Harris	Reid	Clarke	Phillips	Froggatt
		15/10	37,340	*17*		15			*Stamps 86p*	*Webster*	*Poppitt*	*Howe*	*Ward*	*Cushlow*	*Musson*	*Harrison*	*Powell*	*Stamps*	*Steel*	*McLaren*
									Ref: A Bond (Fulham)	England's game at Cardiff deprives Pompey of Dickinson, but Rams are still outclassed. Clarke and Harris combine to let Reid scoop home, then Harris' fine cross is finished by Clarke. Harris then set up Froggatt to seal the points, but Stamps pulls one back when Hindmarsh handles.										
13	A	WEST BROM		5	L		**0-3**	0-2		Butler	Hindmarsh	Ferrier	Scoular	Thompson	Dickinson	**Dawson**	Pickett	Froggatt	Barlow	Parker
		22/10	*40,808*	*8*		15			*Inwood 9, Williams 40, Elliott 62*	*Sanders*	*Pemberton*	*Millard*	*Kennedy*	*Vernon*	*Ryan*	*Elliott*	*Williams*	*Walsh*	*Smith*	*Inwood*
									Ref: F Fiander (Buckingham)	Wolves finally slip at Man U, but patched-up Pompey – Reid and Phillips (flu) Harris and Clarke (injured) – fail to profit. This is the Champs' first game here since '39. With the wind, Inwood's corner goes straight in, then Williams bundles home. Elliott waltzes round Butler to seal it.										
14	H	MANCHESTER U		5	D		0-0	0-0		Butler	Hindmarsh	Ferrier	Scoular	**Spence**	Dickinson	Harris	Pickett	Clarke	Phillips	Froggatt
		29/10	41,098	*3*		16				*Crompton*	*Carey*	*Aston*	*Warner*	*Chilton*	*Cockburn*	*Delaney*	*Bogan*	*Rowley*	*Pearson*	*Mitten*
									Ref: W Ling (Cambridge)	Pompey draft in 23-year-old reserve Spence for his debut. In an interesting match, Phillips went closest, firing just wide early on, but in the second half a series of scrambles see Pompey lucky to survive. Championship ties are on sale, priced 7s 4d, at Landports Drapery Bazaar.										
15	A	CHELSEA		5	W		4-1	2-1	Froggatt 7, 80, Clarke 32, 68	Butler	Hindmarsh	Ferrier	Scoular	Spence	Dickinson	Harris	Reid	Clarke	Phillips	Froggatt
		5/11	*31,650*	*12*		18			*Billington 14*	*Medhurst*	*Bathgate*	*Hughes*	*Armstrong*	*Harris*	*Macauley*	*Gray*	*Billington*	*Bentley*	*Goulden*	*Williams*
									Ref: E Baker (Epsom)	Thousands of Pompey fans brave the wet, then celebrate by letting off fireworks. Froggatt's deflection opens, only for Billington to burst through. Clarke nets after Froggatt and Phillips see shots blocked. Froggatt wows the England selectors, setting up Clarke, then wrapping it up.										
16	H	STOKE		6	D		0-0	0-0		Butler	Hindmarsh	Ferrier	Scoular	Spence	Dickinson	Harris	Reid	Clarke	Phillips	Froggatt
		12/11	33,257	*17*		19				*Herod*	*Watkin*	*McCue*	*Mountford F*	*Franklin*	*Sellars*	*Mountford G*	*Bowyer*	*Godwin*	*Johnstone*	*Malkin*
									Ref: A Tolley (Worcester)	Before the Lord Mayor and Monty in 'civvies' for the day, Pompey fail to make their superiority count. Dickinson – left out of the England team – is on-song, but over-elaboration costs chances. Harris lobs the keeper, but Scoular had handled, then Malkin hits a post for Stoke late on.										
17	A	BURNLEY		7	L		1-2	0-1	Barlow 67	Butler	Hindmarsh	Ferrier	Scoular	Spence	Dickinson	Harris	Reid	Clarke	Barlow	Froggatt
		19/11	*28,541*	*5*		19			*Morris 18, Potts 61*	*Strong*	*Woodruff*	*Mather*	*Attwell*	*Cummings*	*Bray*	*Chew*	*Morris*	*Spencer*	*Potts*	*Hays*
									Ref: N Hillier (Northampton)	The Turf Moor jinx returns, as a poor first-half display costs dear. Early on Pompey appeal in vain for offside, but Hays is free to cross for Morris, then as the visitors step up the pace, Potts makes it two from a corner after hitting the bar. Barlow pulled one back from Harris's cross.										
18	H	SUNDERLAND		7	D		2-2	2-0	Clarke 20, Harris 24	Butler	**Stephen**	Ferrier	**Elder**	Spence	Dickinson	Harris	Reid	**Ekner**	Clarke	Froggatt
		26/11	36,707	*8*		20			*Shackleton 47, Broadis 48*	*Mapson*	*Stelling*	*Hudgell*	*McLain*	*Walsh*	*Wright A*	*Wright T*	*Broadis*	*Davis*	*Shackleton*	*Reynolds*
									Ref: S Law (West Bromwich)	Spence's slip lets in Shackleton, then Broadis nets Reynolds' cross from point blank as Sunderland rally. Earlier Froggatt's deflected cross fell kindly for Clarke, then Swede Ekner – over here on business – set up Harris Reynolds' cut head meant he had to go off despite his protests.										
19	A	LIVERPOOL		7	D		2-2	1-1	Harris 33, Clarke 65	Butler	Hindmarsh	Ferrier	Scoular	Spence	Dickinson	Harris	Ekner	Clarke	Phillips	Froggatt
		3/12	*44,851*	*1*		21			*Done 29, 49*	*Sidlow*	*Lambert*	*Spicer*	*Taylor*	*Hughes*	*Jones*	*Liddell*	*Baron*	*Done*	*Fagan*	*Brierley*
									Ref: G Iliffe (Leicester)	Pompey reassert their title credentials on a pitch so sodden the toss took place by the touchline. Done nods Pool ahead, only for Harris to level with a cross-shot. Done's drive made it 2-1, then Butler has to have mud cleared from his eye, before Clarke levels, seizing on a lucky rebound.										
20	H	ARSENAL		7	W		2-1	0-1	Clarke 78, Froggatt 83	Butler	Hindmarsh	Ferrier	Spence	Flewin	Dickinson	Harris	Ekner	Clarke	Phillips	Froggatt
		10/12	39,527	*4*		23			*Goring 4*	*Platt*	*Barnes*	*Smith*	*Forbes*	*Compton L*	*Mercer*	*Cox*	*Logie*	*Goring*	*Lewis*	*Roper*
									Ref: P Annette (Basingstoke)	A first home win in six weeks, but Arsenal are unlucky. Scoular has to rest his knee, but Flewin returns after an appendix op. Goring nets from close in, but then Gunners fail to capitalise. Clarke glances in Harris's cross and Froggatt wins it when the ball squirts to him from Harris.										
21	H	NEWCASTLE		7	W		1-0	1-0	Clarke 3	Butler	Hindmarsh	Ferrier	Spence	Flewin	Dickinson	Harris	Clarke	Ekner	Phillips	Froggatt
		17/12	30,455	*13*		25				*Garbutt*	*Graham*	*Batty*	*Dodgin*	*Brennan*	*Crowe*	*Walker*	*Houghton*	*Milburn*	*Robledo*	*Mitchell*
									Ref: H Williams (London)	Early on, Hindmarsh's cross deceives Garbutt in the wind and Batty's clearance goes in off Clarke. Milburn and Robledo both go close as Magpies rally, then a cross pole-axes Flewin, who is motionless for a minute as the game goes on. Graham is spoken to for a foul on Froggatt.										

LEAGUE DIVISION 1

Manager: Bob Jackson

SEASON 1949-50

No	Date		Att	Pos	Pt	F-A	H-T	Scorers, Times, and Referees	1	2	3	4	5	6	7	8	9	10	11
22	A	BLACKPOOL		7	L	1-2	1-1	Harris 25	Butler	Hindmarsh	Ferrier	Spence	Flewin	Dickinson	Harris	Clarke	Reid	Phillips	Froggatt
	24/12		*25,953*	*3*	25			*McCall 12, 67*	*Farm*	*Shimwell*	*Garnett*	*Johnston*	*Hayward*	*Kelly*	*Matthews*	*McCall*	*Mortensen*	*McIntosh*	*Wardle*
								Ref: L Thompson (Worksop)	Pool complete a famous double, as McCall nods home Matthews' cross early on. Pompey weather the storm and level when Harris evades a tackle and deftly scores from 18 yards. McCall converts Mortensen's clever pass to win it, and leaders Liverpool are now five points distant.										
23	A	CHARLTON		6	W	2-1	1-0	Phillips 42, Froggatt 62	Butler	Hindmarsh	Ferrier	Scoular	Flewin	Dickinson	Harris	Clarke	Ekner	Phillips	Froggatt
	26/12		*37,539*	*19*	27			*Vaughan 85*	*Bartram*	*Cambell*	*Lock*	*Forbes*	*Allison*	*Ufton*	*Hurst*	*O'Linn*	*Vaughan*	*Purves*	*Fenton*
								Ref: E Crook (Abingdon)	Charlton's late rally nearly steals a point after Phillips trumps Sam Bartram with a 'grand' shot on the interval, then Froggatt's corner goes straight in. Ike Clarke always worried young Charlton centre-half Malcolm Allison, but Vaughan's well-placed shot set up a tense finale.										
24	H	CHARLTON		4	W	1-0	0-0	Harris 46	Butler	Hindmarsh	Ferrier	Scoular	Flewin	Dickinson	Harris	Delapenha	Clarke	Phillips	Froggatt
	27/12		43,650	*20*	29				*Bartram*	*Campbell*	*Lock*	*Revell*	*Phipps*	*Brown*	*Fell*	*O'Linn*	*Vaughan*	*Lumley*	*Fenton*
								Ref: E Crook (Abingdon)	An electric train strike stops hundreds of Charlton fans from getting to Fratton, missing a spirited display by their team, but Harris nods the winner after good work by Froggatt, Phillips and Clarke. The game suffers as a spectacle as the players tire after a third game in four days.										
25	H	MIDDLESBROUGH		5	D	1-1	0-0	Froggatt 48	Butler	Hindmarsh	Ferrier	Scoular	Flewin	Dickinson	Harris	Delapenha	Clarke	Phillips	Froggatt
	31/12		33,364	*12*	30			*McKennan 61*	*Ugolini*	*Dicks*	*Dale*	*Hardwick*	*Whitaker*	*Gordon*	*Linacre*	*Mannion*	*McKennan*	*McCrae*	*Walker*
								Ref: W Ling (Cambridge)	Watched by Norwich's boss – cup opponents next week – Phillips misses a sitter and Harris has a goal ruled out for offside. McCrae hit a post against the run of play, before Froggatt finally scored in a goalmouth mêlée. Boro level when McKennan races away to lift the ball over Butler.										
26	A	EVERTON		4	W	2-1	0-1	Phillips 62, Harris 73	Butler	Hindmarsh	Ferrier	Scoular	Flewin	Dickinson	Harris	Reid	Clarke	Phillips	Parker
	14/1		*50,421*	*19*	32			*Grant 37*	*Burnett*	*Moore*	*Hedley*	*Grant*	*Salver*	*Lello*	*Buckie*	*Wainwright*	*Catterick*	*Farrell*	*Eglington*
								Ref: W Rogers (Birmingham)	Jaded from their Norwich trip on Thursday, Pompey start slowly and Toffees lead when Grant fires home. Reid is off for 15 minutes, but in the meantime Phillips nodded in a free-kick. A home fan throws something at the referee and the police intervene, before Harris's first-time finish.										
27	H	HUDDERSFIELD		4	W	4-0	1-0	Wh'ler 30 (og), Reid 60, Fr'ggatt 67, 75	Butler	Hindmarsh	Ferrier	Scoular	Flewin	Dickinson	Harris	Reid	Clarke	Phillips	Froggatt
	21/1		29,746	*18*	34				*Wheeler*	*Gallogly*	*Stewart*	*Battye*	*Boot*	*Morgan*	*McKenna*	*Lynn*	*Burke*	*Nightingale*	*Metcalfe*
								Ref: H Pearce (Luton)	The Admiral of the Fleet joins Monty in the Directors Box as Wheeler sinks Terriers' hopes by dropping Froggatt's cross over the line. The keeper was also injured, only resuming after treatment, but he couldn't deny Reid, then Froggatt from close range and direct from a corner.										
28	A	BOLTON		4	L	0-1	0-0		Butler	Hindmarsh	Ferrier	Scoular	Flewin	Dickinson	Parker	Reid	Clarke	Phillips	Froggatt
	4/2		*32,441*	*17*	34			*Lofthouse 63*	*Hanson*	*Roberts*	*Banks*	*Barrass*	*Aspinall*	*Howe*	*McShane*	*Moir*	*Lofthouse*	*Bradley*	*Langton*
								Ref: E Vickery (Bristol)	Reid's saved penalty, after he was fouled by Barrass in the eighth minute, proves costly and numerous other chances go begging. Lofthouse nods the winner in a furious goalmouth scramble, then Reid fires over when well placed and Phillips hits the crossbar in the last ten minutes.										
29	A	WOLVERHAMPTON		5	L	0-1	0-1		Butler	Rookes	Ferrier	Scoular	Flewin	Dickinson	Harris	Pickett	Clarke	Phillips	Froggatt
	18/2		*46,679*	*7*	34			*McLean 7*	*Williams*	*Kelly*	*Pritchard*	*Baxter*	*Shorthouse*	*Wright*	*Smith*	*Walker*	*McLean*	*Swinbourne*	*Mullen*
								Ref: G Clark (London)	Pompey slip six points off the pace as makeshift Wolves – 14 stone full-back McLean was playing up front – snatch the points. McLean soon makes his weight count, nodding home Mullen's corner. Pompey rarely looked like saving it, but Williams had to be at his best to deny Harris.										
30	H	BIRMINGHAM		4	W	2-0	0-0	Harris 47, 89	Butler	Rookes	Ferrier	Scoular	Thompson	Dickinson	Harris	Pickett	**Higham**	Phillips	**Bennett**
	25/2		28,429	*22*	36				*Merrick*	*Duckhouse*	*Green*	*Dornan*	*Badham*	*McKee*	*Berry*	*Stewart*	*Dailey*	*Harris*	*Roberts*
								Ref: W Edwards (Yeovil)	Royal Marine Higham (18) is picked after just two reserve games and he helps break Birmingham, setting up Harris to run across the face of goal and angle in. Earlier Pickett hit a post and only Merrick's agility kept the score down, although he misjudged Harris's lob at the death.										
31	A	DERBY		7	L	1-2	1-0	Pickett 42	Butler	Rookes	Ferrier	Scoular !	Thompson	Dickinson	Harris	Pickett	Reid	Phillips	Froggatt
	8/3		***17,713***	*10*	36			*Stamps 68, 85*	*Townsend*	*Mozley*	*Parr*	*Ward*	*Oliver*	*Musson*	*Mynad*	*Morris !*	*Stamps*	*Steel*	*Powell*
								Ref: A Bond (London)	Scoular's sending off for a kick and Morris's red card for retaliation overshadow a game Pompey should have won. Pickett grabs the lead with a fine shot, but Stamps bundles Butler and ball over the line, then profits from some sloppy defending. Scoular must await the wrath of the FA.										

No	Ven	Opponent	Att	Pos	Res	FT	HT	Scorers, Times, Referees	1	2	3	4	5	6	7	8	9	10	11
32	H	BURNLEY		5	W	2-1	2-0	Froggatt 1, Clarke 25	Butler	Hindmarsh	Ferrier	Scoular	Flewin	Dickinson	Harris	Pickett	Clarke	Phillips	Froggatt
	11/3		**26,728**	*9*	38			*Spencer 83*	*Strong*	*Hayes*	*Woodruff*	*Bray*	*Cummings*	*Attwell*	*Hays*	*Potts*	*Spencer*	*Morris*	*Shannon*
								Ref: N Hillier (Northampton)	The small crowd suggests Pompey's title dream is dying and they make heavy weather of this game. Clarets are not a vintage and haven't won since December. Froggatt's acute angle shot looks harmless, but it squirms in, then Clarke nets after a scramble. Spencer ensures a tense finish.										
33	A	SUNDERLAND		5	D	1-1	1-1	Bennett 38	Butler	Hindmarsh	Ferrier	Scoular	Flewin	Dickinson	Harris	Pickett	Reid	Clarke	Bennett
	18/3		*44,591*	*4*	39			*Davis 41*	*Mapson*	*Stelling*	*Hudgell*	*Watson*	*Hall*	*Wright A*	*Wright T*	*Broadis*	*Davis*	*Shackleton*	*Reynolds*
								Ref: S Laws (West Bromwich)	Sunderland's title bid, on the back of an eight-match unbeaten run, is slowed by Pompey who defy the formbook and go ahead when Reid puts Bennett away to beat his man and score. Davis hooks home the equaliser from a narrow angle as Ferrier misjudges a bouncing ball in the wind.										
34	H	CHELSEA		4	W	4-0	3-0	Reid 11, 40, 62, Harris 38	Butler	Hindmarsh	Ferrier	Scoular	Flewin	Dickinson	Harris	Reid	Clarke	Pickett	Froggatt
	25/3		28,574	*12*	41				*Medhurst*	*Winter*	*Hughes*	*Armstrong*	*Harris*	*Mitchell*	*Gray*	*Jenkings*	*Bentley*	*Williams*	*Campbell*
								Ref: E Baker (Manchester)	Huddersfield's win over Man U opens up the title race, as Pompey cruise past jaded semi-final replay losers Chelsea. Today's hero is Reid who claims a headed hat-trick, from centres by Froggatt, Dickinson and Harris respectively. Harris's cool head punishes Medhurst's rash rush.										
35	A	STOKE		5	W	1-0	0-0	Harris 50	Butler	Hindmarsh	Ferrier	Scoular	Flewin	Dickinson	Harris	Reid	Clarke	Pickett	Froggatt
	1/4		*26,521*	*15*	43				*Wilkinson*	*Watson*	*McCue*	*Mountford F*	*Franklin*	*Sellars*	*Malkin*	*Bowyer*	*Mountford G*	*Johnston*	*Oscroft*
								Ref: A Tolley (Worcester)	United drop another point as Harris settles this game when the keeper misjudges Froggatt's corner. Stoke look the livelier early on, but once Pompey go ahead there is only one winner – despite losing Flewin for ten minutes – delighting a small band of bell ringing and rattling fans.										
36	H	FULHAM		4	W	3-0	1-0	Harris 18, 49, Froggatt 57	Butler	Hindmarsh	Ferrier	Scoular	Spence	Dickinson	Harris	Reid	Clarke	Pickett	Froggatt
	7/4		39,342	*14*	45				*Kelly*	*Freeman*	*Bacuzzi*	*Quested*	*Taylor*	*Beasley*	*Stevens*	*Thomas*	*Campbell*	*Jezzard*	*Hinshelwood*
								Ref: E Vickery (Bristol)	Harris surely plays himself into England contention, bewildering Bacuzzi. First he flashes a shot into the roof of the net from an acute angle, then draws Kelly and slots home, after being put clear by Clarke. Finally he sets up Froggatt for a header which had the power of a shot.										
37	H	WEST BROM		5	L	0-1	0-0		Butler	Hindmarsh	Ferrier	Scoular	Spence	Dickinson	Harris	Phillips	Clarke	Pickett	Froggatt
	8/4		33,903	*15*	45			*Ryan 75*	*Sanders*	*Pemberton*	*Millard*	*Kennedy*	*Vernon*	*Ryan*	*Gordon*	*Smith*	*Walsh*	*Dudley*	*Lee*
								Ref: F Fiander (Loudwater)	Pompey's title hopes look dead after Baggies master the blustery conditions. With a defence well marshalled by Irish cap Vernon, they knock Pompey out of their stride, but it is still a surprise when Ryan's 30-yard cross-shot seals it. Clarke nearly saved it late on, but shaved the bar.										
38	A	FULHAM		3	W	1-0	1-0	Clarke 13	Butler	Hindmarsh	Ferrier	Scoular	Spence	Dickinson	Harris	Delapenha	Clarke	Pickett	Froggatt
	10/4		*24,812*	*16*	47				*Slack*	*Freeman*	*Bacuzzi*	*Quested*	*Pavitt*	*Taylor*	*Hinshelwood*	*Campbell*	*Rowley*	*Thomas*	*McDonald*
								Ref: E Vickery (Bristol)	The title may yet stay at Fratton after this lucky win which sees Ferrier miss an early penalty after Freeman handled. Pickett and Froggatt combined to set up Clarke who beat Pavitt before scoring. Backed by a stiff breeze in the second half Fulham press, but Butler is on form.										
39	A	MANCHESTER U		1	W	2-0	0-0	Reid 84, Froggatt 89	Butler	Hindmarsh	Ferrier	Scoular	Spence	Thompson	Harris	Reid	Clarke	Phillips	Froggatt
	15/4		*46,709*	*2*	49				*Crompton*	*McNulty*	*Ball*	*Whitefoot*	*Chilton*	*Cockburn*	*Delaney*	*Pearson*	*Rowley*	*Downie*	*Mitten*
								Ref: W Ling (Stapleford)	Two late goals transform Pompey's prospects. Without Dickinson (England duty) and Flewin (hospital), stout defending and opportunism are the key. Reid feeds off Clarke's flick, then Froggatt nods in Scoular's cross. Liverpool and Sunderland falter leaving Pompey in pole position.										
40	H	LIVERPOOL		1	W	2-1	0-0	Reid 61, Froggatt 80	Butler	Hindmarsh	Ferrier	Scoular	Spence	Dickinson	Harris	Reid	Clarke	Phillips	Froggatt
	22/4		47,507	*4*	51			*Stubbins 52*	*Minshull*	*Lambert*	*Spicer*	*Taylor*	*Hughes*	*Jones*	*Watkinson*	*Balmer*	*Stubbins*	*Fagen*	*Liddell*
								Ref: G Iliffe (Leicester)	Queues form at 8am, while Pool have a pre-Cup Final Wembley trip en route. Stubbins revives Reds' double hopes, deflecting Liddell's lob, but once Reid heads in Harris' free-kick Pompey take over. Scoular's far-post cross is met by Froggatt's head; just two more points are needed.										
41	A	ARSENAL		1	L	0-2	0-1		Butler	Hindmarsh	Ferrier	Thompson	Spence	Dickinson	Harris	Reid	Pickett	Phillips	Froggatt
	3/5		***63,124***	*8*	51			*Goring 25, 80*	*Swindin*	*Scott*	*Barnes*	*Forbes*	*Compton L*	*Mercer*	*Cox*	*Logie*	*Goring*	*Lewis*	*Compton D*
								Ref: P Annette (Basingstoke)	Injuries rob Pompey of Clarke (toe) and Flewin (hip), while Scoular is controversially banned. They are always second best to the FA Cup winners wearing their Wembley yellow. A late rally nearly earns a point, after Goring had nodded Gunners in front, then slotted past Butler.										
42	H	ASTON VILLA		1	W	5-1	2-0	Thompson 1, 72, Reid 26, 48, 80	Butler	Hindmarsh	Ferrier	Spence	Flewin	Dickinson	Harris	Reid	Thompson	Phillips	Froggatt
	6/5		42,295	*12*	53			*Dorsett 88p*	*Rutherford*	*Parkes*	*Dorsett*	*Powell*	*Martin*	*Moss*	*Dixon*	*Gibson*	*Craddock*	*Edwards*	*Goffin*
		Home	Away					Ref: A Blythe (London)	Scoular is still suspended and Clarke injured, so centre-half Thompson fills in up front and nets Froggatt's pass after just 20 seconds! By the time Reid nods the fifth – his hat-trick – the title flag has already been hoisted again. Dorsett's penalty after Hindmarsh handles is a footnote.										
Average		37,393	37,797																

LEAGUE DIVISION 1 (CUP-TIES) Manager: Bob Jackson SEASON 1949-50

FA Cup

Rd	Venue	Opponent / Date / Att	Pos	Res	F-A	H-T	Scorers, Times, and Referees	1	2	3	4	5	6	7	8	9	10	11
3	H	NORWICH	5	D	1-1	1-0	Delapenha 28	Butler	Hindmarsh	Ferrier	Scoular	Flewin	Dickinson	Harris	Delapenha	Clarke	Phillips	Pickett
	7/1	42,059 *3S:4*					*Kinsey 60*	*Nethercott*	*Duffy*	*Lewis*	*Pickwick*	*Low*	*Armes*	*Gavin*	*Kinsey*	*Ashman*	*Ryder*	*Eyre*
							Ref: A Bond (London)											

City fan Tom Davies (17) cycled to Portsmouth overnight and is rewarded with a return on the team bus and a famous draw. Wearing special silk shirts, City fell behind, although Delapenha's header seemed more hand, but Kinsey nipped in to level as Butler stooped for a back-pass.

Rd	Venue	Opponent / Date / Att	Pos	Res	F-A	H-T	Scorers, Times, and Referees	1	2	3	4	5	6	7	8	9	10	11
3R	A	NORWICH	5	W	2-0	0-0	Reid 48, 78p	Butler	Hindmarsh	Ferrier	Scoular	Flewin	Dickinson	Harris	Reid	Clarke	Phillips	Froggatt
	12/1	*42,624 3S: 4*						*Nethercott*	*Duffy*	*Lewis*	*Pickwick*	*Low*	*Armes*	*Gavin*	*Kinsey*	*Ashman*	*Ryder*	*Church*
							Ref: A Bond (London)											

Hundreds of Pompey fans arrive late after a special train is held up. The start is also delayed, to mend a hole to the net! Canaries play well in the first half – Ryder blazes over – but once Reid spins and hooks in, the minnows resolve is broken. It's a record attendance for Carrow Road.

Rd	Venue	Opponent / Date / Att	Pos	Res	F-A	H-T	Scorers, Times, and Referees	1	2	3	4	5	6	7	8	9	10	11
4	H	GRIMSBY	4	W	5-0	2-0	Froggatt 10, 77, Clarke 18, 71, [Phillips 89]	Butler	Hindmarsh	Ferrier	Scoular	Flewin	Dickinson	Parker	Reid	Clarke	Phillips	Froggatt
	28/1	39,364 *2:10*						*Bircham*	*Hamby*	*Fisher*	*Duthie*	*McMillan*	*Johnston*	*Hair*	*Cairns*	*Briggs*	*Barney*	*McStay*
							Ref: R Burgess (Reading)											

Poor Mariners are all at sea once Froggatt's header off the underside is adjudged to have gone in. Clarke profited as Reid missed his kick then Butler hurt his wrist as Briggs hit him at full speed, but he still managed to save. That was Town's last chance as Pompey made class tell.

Rd	Venue	Opponent / Date / Att	Pos	Res	F-A	H-T	Scorers, Times, and Referees	1	2	3	4	5	6	7	8	9	10	11
5	A	MANCHESTER U	4	D	3-3	0-2	Clarke 48, Parker 49, Ferrier 68p	Butler	Hindmarsh	Ferrier	Scoular	Flewin	Dickinson	Harris	Clarke	Froggatt	Phillips	Parker
	11/2	*53,688* *2*					*Mitten 24, 51p, Pearson 40*	*Lancaster*	*Carey*	*Aston*	*Warner*	*Chilton*	*Cockburn*	*Delaney*	*Bogan*	*Rowley*	*Pearson*	*Mitten*
							Ref: R Lease (Nottingham)											

Watched by the Scots selectors, United forge ahead – not before Phillips had hit a post – by Mitten's shot and Pearson's header. Clarke scores from close range, then '39 veteran Parker levels from Harris' centre. Ferrier atones for his handball by keeping cool after Chilton handled.

Rd	Venue	Opponent / Date / Att	Pos	Res	F-A	H-T	Scorers, Times, and Referees	1	2	3	4	5	6	7	8	9	10	11
5R	H	MANCHESTER U	4	L	1-3	1-2	Harris 42	Butler	Hindmarsh	Ferrier	Scoular	Flewin	Dickinson	Harris	Clarke	Froggatt	Phillips	Parker
	15/2	49,962 *2*					*Mitten 11, Downie 24, Delaney 46*	*Feehan*	*Carey*	*Aston*	*Warner*	*Chilton*	*Cockburn*	*Delaney*	*Bogan*	*Rowley*	*Downie*	*Mitten*
							Ref: R Lease (Nottingham)											

Downie – a £16,500 reserve, in for the injured Pearson – makes the difference. His pass sets up Mitten, then his drive nearly breaks the net. A Harris run and shot reduces the arrears, but within a minute of the restart Delaney rams in from close and United are off to Chelsea in round 6.

Charity Shield

Venue	Opponent / Date / Att	Res	F-A	H-T	Scorers, Times, and Referees	1	2	3	4	5	6	7	8	9	10	11
N	WOLVERHAMPTON	D	1-1	1-0	Reid 32	Butler	Hindmarsh	Ferrier	Scoular	Thompson	Dickinson	Harris	Reid	Clarke	Barlow	Froggatt
19/10	*25,000*				*Hancocks 64p*	*Parsons*	*Kelly*	*Springthorpe*	*Russell*	*Shorthouse*	*Crook*	*Hancocks*	*Smyth*	*Pye*	*Dunne*	*Mullen*
	(at Highbury)				Ref: A Blythe (London)											

The Charity Shield comes home with Pompey, but will be off to Molineux in six months, after Ferrier is adjudged to have handled. Wolves don't appeal and the crowd laugh at the award. Earlier Reid netted with a fierce shot. Pompey sold £135-worth of tickets to Wolves' £35.

Tour Match

Venue	Opponent / Date / Att	Res	F-A	H-T	Scorers, Times, and Referees	1	2	3	4	5	6	7	8	9	10	11
H	DANISH NAT'NAL XI	W	6-2	4-0	Clarke 14, 25, Reid 17, 30, 57, [Froggatt 62]	Butler	Hindmarsh	Ferrier	Scoular	Flewin	Thompson	Dawson	Reid	Clarke	Phillips	Froggatt
22/9	*18,500*				*Holm 70, 78*	*Nielsen E*	*Koppen*	*Petersen*	*Nielsen S*	*Andersen*	*Jensen*	*Frandsen*	*Rechendorf*	*Holm*	*Lundberg*	*Lyngsaa*
					Ref: G Reader (Southampton)											

Pompey make short work of the Danes, who impress with their technical ability. However, only keeper Nielsen kept the score respectable. Clarke and Reid combine well up front. The crowd has the novelty of seeing a substitute come on as Bennike replaces Lyngsaa at half-time.

		Home					Away					
	P	W	D	L	F	A	W	D	L	F	A	Pts
1 PORTSMOUTH	42	12	7	2	44	15	10	2	9	30	23	53
2 Wolves	42	11	8	2	47	21	9	5	7	29	28	53
3 Sunderland	42	14	6	1	50	23	7	4	10	33	39	52
4 Manchester U	42	11	5	5	42	20	7	9	5	27	24	50
5 Newcastle	42	14	4	3	49	23	5	8	8	28	32	50
6 Arsenal	42	12	4	5	48	24	7	7	7	31	31	49
7 Blackpool	42	10	8	3	29	14	7	7	7	17	21	49
8 Liverpool	42	10	7	4	37	23	7	7	7	27	31	48
9 Middlesbro	42	14	2	5	37	18	6	5	10	22	30	47
10 Burnley	42	9	7	5	23	17	7	6	8	17	23	45
11 Derby	42	11	5	5	46	26	6	5	10	23	35	44
12 Aston Villa	42	10	7	4	31	19	5	5	11	30	42	42
13 Chelsea	42	7	7	7	31	30	5	9	7	27	35	40
14 West Brom	42	9	7	5	28	16	5	5	11	19	37	40
15 Huddersfield	42	11	4	6	34	22	3	5	13	18	51	37
16 Bolton	42	10	5	6	34	22	0	9	12	11	37	34
17 Fulham	42	8	6	7	24	19	2	8	11	17	35	34
18 Everton	42	6	8	7	24	20	4	6	11	18	46	34
19 Stoke	42	10	4	7	27	28	1	8	12	18	47	34
20 Charlton	42	7	5	9	33	35	6	1	14	20	30	32
21 Manchester C	42	7	8	6	27	24	1	5	15	9	44	29
22 Birmingham	42	6	8	7	19	24	1	6	14	12	43	28
	924	219	132	111	764	483	111	132	219	483	764	924

Odds & ends

Double wins: (6) Newcastle, Everton, Huddersfield, Birmingham, Chelsea, Charlton.
Double losses: (2) Blackpool, West Brom.

Won from behind: (3) Arsenal (h), Everton (a), Liverpool (h).
Lost from in front: (2) Blackpool (h), Derby (a).

High spots: Thrashing Everton 7-0 at home in September.
Winning at Old Trafford in April against their closest title rivals.
Coming from behind to beat title rivals Liverpool at home in April.
Beating Aston Villa 5-1 at home in the final game to retain the league.

Low spots: Losing 2-3 at home to Blackpool in August. A first home defeat since Boxing day 1947.
Being robbed of an outright Charity Shield win after a suspect penalty.
Losing 1-3 at home to Manchester United in an FA Cup fifth round replay.

Hat-tricks: (4) Reid (3), Harris.
Ever-presents: (2) Butler, Ferrier.
Leading scorer: Clarke (17).

	Appearances			Goals			
	Lge	FA	CS	Lge	FAC	CS	Tot
Barlow, Bert	**2**		1	**1**			**1**
Bennett, Ron	**2**			**1**			**1**
Butler, Ernie	**42**	5	1				
Clarke, Ike	**37**	5	1	**17**	3		**20**
Dawson, James	**1**						
Delapenha, Lindy	**5**	1			1		**1**
Dickinson, Jim	**40**	5	1				
Ekner, Daniel	**5**						
Elder, James	**1**						
Ferrier, Harry	**42**	5	1		1		**1**
Flewin, Reg	**24**	5					
Froggatt, Jack	**39**	4	1	**14**	2		**16**
Harris, Peter	**40**	4	1	**16**	1		**17**
Higham, Peter	**1**						
Hindmarsh, Bill	**34**	5	1				
Parker, Cliff	**3**	3			1		**1**
Phillips, Len	**34**	5		**5**	1		**6**
Pickett, Reg	**14**	1		**1**			**1**
Reid, Duggie	**27**	2	1	**16**	2	1	**19**
Rookes, Phil	**3**						
Scoular, Jimmy	**36**	5	1				
Spence, Bill	**16**						
Stephen, James	**1**						
Thompson, Bill	**9**		1	**2**			**2**
Yeuell, Jasper	**4**						
(own-goals)				**1**			**1**
25 players used	**462**	**55**	**11**	**74**	**12**	**1**	**87**

LIST OF SUBSCRIBERS

VOTES FOR THE MOST IMPORTANT POMPEY PLAYER 1948-1950

Subscriber	Vote
Adlam, Ray	Duggie Reid
Allen, Mark	Jack Froggatt
Barnard, Mike	Jimmy Dickinson
Benzeval, Mike	Peter Harris
Boynton, Paul	Jimmy Dickinson
Brett, E Mr	Peter Harris
Byrne, Steve	Duggie Reid
Cheatle, Alan	Peter Harris
Coates, George	Jimmy Scoular
Cowley, Patrick L	Peter Harris
Cully, J D	Jimmy Dickinson
Dicken, Roger	Len Phillips
Gardner, John	Len Phillips
Hatcher, Stephen Mr	Jimmy Dickinson
Hinks, Philip H	Jimmy Dickinson
Hood, Peter H	Duggie Reid
Howe-Haysom, Tony	Len Phillips
Hudson, R C	Peter Harris
Jenkins, Brian	Peter Harris
Kent P	Jimmy Dickinson
Kidd A K	Peter Harris
Kirby, Mark	Duggie Reid
Larcombe, Keith	Ernie Butler
Millar, Chris	
Nicholls, Simon	Jimmy Dickinson
Nottage, Mike	Peter Harris
Oliver, Keith	Peter Harris
Page, Patrick	Jimmy Scoular
Pelling, Daphne Miss	Jimmy Dickinson
Porter, Andy	
Prowting, Mr & Mrs Brian	Reg Flewin
Quick, David John Mr	Jack Froggatt
Reed, George Thomas	Jimmy Scoular
Richardson, Chris	Duggie Reid
Rigby, J R Mr	Jack Froggatt
Robinson, Ric	Jack Froggatt
Roe, B Mr	Duggie Reid
Stanley, R R Mr	Len Phillips
Starr, Don	
Stewart, Ham	Peter Harris
Tollerfield, Trevor	Jimmy Dickinson
Tomalin, Steve	The whole team
Turner, D E Mr	Peter Harris
Veal, June	Jimmy Dickinson
Wateridge, Shirley Mrs	Jack Froggatt
Waters, John S	Jimmy Dickinson
Wheeler, Mike	Peter Harris
White, Ian M	
Wilson, Richard C	Peter Harris

MOST IMPORTANT POMPEY PLAYER 1948-50
(7 different players received votes)

1st	Peter Harris
2nd	Jimmy Dickinson
3rd	Duggie Reid
4th	Jack Froggatt
5th	Len Phillips